TRANSFORMER

Praise for the series:

It was only a matter of time before a clever publisher realized that there is an audience for whom *Exile on Main Street* or *Electric Ladyland* are as significant and worthy of study as *The Catcher in the Rye* or *Middlemarch* . . . The series . . . is freewheeling and eclectic, ranging from minute rock-geek analysis to idiosyncratic personal celebration
—*The New York Times Book Review*

Ideal for the rock geek who thinks liner notes just aren't enough
—*Rolling Stone*

One of the coolest publishing imprints on the planet —*Bookslut*

These are for the insane collectors out there who appreciate fantastic design, well-executed thinking, and things that make your house look cool. Each volume in this series takes a seminal album and breaks it down in startling minutiae. We love these. We are huge nerds —*Vice*

A brilliant series . . . each one a work of real love —*NME* (UK)

Passionate, obsessive, and smart —*Nylon*

Religious tracts for the rock 'n' roll faithful —*Boldtype*

[A] consistently excellent series —*Uncut* (UK)

We . . . aren't naive enough to think that we're your only source for reading about music (but if we had our way . . . watch out). For those of you who really like to know everything there is to know about an album, you'd do well to check out Bloomsbury's "33 1/3" series of books —*Pitchfork*

For reviews of individual titles in the series, please visit our blog at 333so ⬛ **oomsbury.com/ musican** ⬛ **ooks Like us on** ⬛ **books**

For a c ⬛ k of this book

Forthcoming in the series:

and many more…

Transformer

Ezra Furman

BLOOMSBURY ACADEMIC
NEW YORK · LONDON · OXFORD · NEW DELHI · SYDNEY

BLOOMSBURY ACADEMIC
Bloomsbury Publishing Inc
1385 Broadway, New York, NY 10018, USA
50 Bedford Square, London, WC1B 3DP, UK
29 Earlsfort Terrace, Dublin 2, Ireland

BLOOMSBURY, BLOOMSBURY ACADEMIC and the Diana logo are
trademarks of Bloomsbury Publishing Plc

First published in the United States of America 2018
Reprinted 2018 (twice), 2019, 2020, 2021, 2022 (twice), 2024

Bloomsbury Publishing Inc does not have any control over, or responsibility
for, any third-party websites referred to or in this book. All internet
addresses given in this book were correct at the time of going to press. The
author and publisher regret any inconvenience caused if addresses have
changed or sites have ceased to exist, but can accept no responsibility for
any such changes.

A catalog record for this book is available from the Library of Congress.

ISBN: PB: 978-1-5013-2305-8
ePDF: 978-1-5013-2306-5
eBook: 978-1-5013-2307-2

Series: 33$\frac{1}{3}$

Typeset by Deanta Global Publishing Services, Chennai, India
Printed and bound in Great Britain

To find out more about our authors and books visit www.bloomsbury.com
and sign up for our newsletters.

Contents

CONTENTS

Fuck You Leave Me Alone
Don't Read My Book

Let me clear the air from the outset: I don't think *Transformer* is the greatest record ever made. I don't think it's the greatest record of the seventies. I wouldn't even pick it as the greatest album of 1972. After all, both *Pink Moon* by Nick Drake and *Sail Away* by Randy Newman were released in 1972 and those are perfect albums. Even if you restrict your search to the best rock 'n' roll album of that year, most would probably turn to the Rolling Stones' *Exile on Main Street* or David Bowie's *The Rise and Fall of Ziggy Stardust & the Spiders From Mars*. If you're looking for a worshipful chronicling of *Transformer*'s creation and unassailable greatness, you got the wrong book. I'm here to break the news that most people's favorite Lou Reed solo album is a deeply flawed work that is disappointing in multiple ways—certainly not the greatest record ever made. But the reason I keep returning to it, even more so than for the pleasure afforded by its best moments, is that it's *interestingly* disappointing. *Transformer*'s failings as an album fascinatingly parallel the failings—personal and artistic—of the man whose name it bears. And Lou Reed is one of the most compelling figures in the rock music canon, not despite his weaknesses, but because of them.

Usually, whether or not you like a record is a simple matter. You can tell as soon as you've heard it. If you like it, you re-listen to it, you talk about it, etc.; if you dislike it, though you might verbally trash it with your friends for a while, pretty soon you move on and forget about it. But then there are certain records where you can't quite decide, records that provoke a reaction that somehow contains both shades of "I adore this" and "I'm not interested." It's not that these records are of middling quality, or that they strike me as average. No, these occasional records that float ambiguously out of the range of my ability to coherently react to them really *bother* me. At the same time that they make me want to love them, they prevent me from doing so by failing to live up to the promise of their better moments.

It's an uncomfortable place to be for a lot of music fans, especially the ones who make a point of having strong opinions about what they listen to. Part of the most commonly invoked archetype of the music collector is that she compulsively categorizes, ranks, and evaluates. When we run into work that provokes in us an ambiguous reaction or is resistant to categorization, many of us are repelled. Not knowing how to take it, we set it aside in favor of music we understand in a more direct way. But once in a while, we end up obsessed, listening and re-listening as though trying to crack its secret code.

Transformer is one of these albums, and for me, it is its ambiguity that elevates it beyond simply being a good record to make it an utterly unforgettable one. What sets

Transformer apart is that ultimately the whole album is in fact *about* ambiguity, and the process of becoming rather than being. It is so uncategorizable in every aspect that even to call it uncategorizable is to suggest a framework that reductively pigeonholes the record. After all, there are plenty of legitimate categories fans use: a glam rock album, an early punk album, a "commercial breakthrough," an album about sexuality or gender—but the thing is that *Transformer* actively aims to land neither inside nor outside any of these categories; not fully. It will inhabit a label for a moment, long enough for you to think you can call it that, and then it will destabilize that label and sneer at you for using it. It is thoroughly noncommittal, a work that, like its author, is so concerned with becoming, transforming, that it doesn't have time to actually fully *be* anything.

In the end, this is what makes it so exciting. If you spend time with *Transformer*, it turns out to be an album about total freedom, a rejection of all terms and categories, a declaration of independence from anything and everything you thought you had to say about it.

And that's why it's the greatest record ever made.

* * *

Another thing to keep in mind while you read this book: I love Lou Reed. I'll act all cool and detached in a lot of these pages; I'm going to display some harsh skepticism and poke holes in Reed's overblown mythos and call him names. Don't be fooled. I'm a desperately fascinated Lou Reed fan, and I cannot get enough of him. I'm of the incorrigible type whose obsession expands beyond the music and attaches to

TRANSFORMER

the artist personally, as if to really know this person would answer deep, urgent questions about myself. I listen to and think about Reed like an adopted child might search for his biological father: first wondering, then researching, then going on a journey to find him, but never reaching the satisfaction that would come with really knowing the absent man who gave him life. I have found my father's old address, his records, his interviews, his life story. I even got to meet him once when I was twenty-one. But truly knowing him remains out of reach.

Even for a more normal, less cripplingly obsessed fan, the question of who Lou Reed really is is a bit of a thorny one. More so than most celebrities, this man's identity is deeply unclear. Of course we never know who a stranger is until we have actually met them, and even then we often come away with very little knowledge of what they are "really like." But regardless of one's "true self," a public figure will at least usually display a coherent outward persona: George W. Bush plays the folksy compassionate conservative, Bill Murray is a semi-reclusive goofy-but-soulful scamp, and so on. We have, at minimum, identifiable meta-personalities for these people, facades they consistently project to the wider world.

With Lou, it's not quite that simple. He introduced himself to the public—albeit not much of a commercially significant public, considering the Velvet Underground's downright depressing initial record sales numbers—as a mid-sixties avant-garde, black-turtlenecked musical visionary, hanging out with Andy Warhol, shooting heroin, having kinky sex, and playing as loudly, atonally, and aggressively as possible.

Yet by 1968 the Velvets were recording tender, at times quasi-spiritual outsider folk-rock, and Reed's vocals had mutated from fuck-you drawl to an achingly tender lilt. Even when they played loud, at the end of their career the Velvet Underground were presenting pretty much traditional, radio-friendly rock 'n' roll (though none of it actually got played on the radio) whose most direct influence was probably pop superstars the Rolling Stones. Lou Reed's solo career is just as beguiling: *Transformer*, his most well-known album by a large measure, paints him as an androgynous glam rocker. But on most subsequent releases he appears as butch and unadorned as possible, repudiating all traces of glam's showy male femininity.

The oxymorons continue: people call Lou Reed's music "punk," but he was at odds with and distant from the media-saturated late-seventies movement that bears that name; rather, he prefigured it and never stuck to its musical or aesthetic ethos. Many, including Lou himself, laud his songs for bringing a literary artfulness to rock songwriting, but he has written an equal or larger number of lyrics that are thoroughly insipid, devoid of almost any content other than rock cliché. Is he just a lifelong outsider, the ultracool criminal of the pop world? If so, what do we make of most of his output in the eighties, in which he reimagined himself as a sober, patriotic, mainstream-radio-courting conservative ready to moralize in song about the deplorable violence in movies and television? He did a goddamn American Express ad in 1985, for goodness' sake.

More than anything, Lou Reed as the public knows him is a man who wears sunglasses. That's pretty much all you can accurately say as a generalized statement. I suppose you can say that he likes playing guitar. So that's what we have here, in broad strokes: a pair of sunglasses that shuts us out, and a guitar that violently attacks us.

As a symbolic prop, those sunglasses seem almost more important than the guitar. What the dark glasses seem to say is, "You don't know me, and you're not going to get to know me." And in many ways, we his audience never did get to know him. Despite the fact that he put out more than thirty records and has had his life chronicled in various prominent biographies, Lou remains elusive, undefined. Ask, and you will be turned away; try to look him in the eyes, and you will see only your own reflection. For some of us, this sort of refusal is exactly what makes us ache to know more.

It's a legitimate stance for a celebrity to ask to be left alone, to say that who he actually is is none of his audience's business. Where it gets tricky with Reed is when he shows us, in his songs and public statements, a surface persona that deliberately and pointedly hints at a more interesting interior, full of secrets we can almost guess. Is my trying to figure out who he is and what he's thinking a needlessly nosy audience overreach? Or is it in fact the intended effect of the work?

A natural everyman-type approach to getting to know an artist would be to start with their most prominent and popular album. Which for Lou Reed, I would argue, despite how much people talk about the Velvet Underground, is actually *Transformer*. It went to #29 on the Billboard 200 Charts in the United States in 1972 and #13 on the UK Album Charts the following year, which for our non-conformist noncommercial hero is exceptionally successful. (1974's *Sally*

Can't Dance actually squeaked into the Top 10, but its legacy is far more compromised than *Transformer*. Most critics, including Reed himself, seem to hate it, and no singles were released from the album.) *Transformer*'s lead single, "Take A Walk on the Wild Side," made it to #16 in the United States and #10 in the United Kingdom. To this day it's the only one of his songs most people have heard, if they have heard any.[1]

Yet, what does the neophyte listener encounter upon dipping into Reed's career via this reportedly most listener-friendly album? What did I encounter at age nineteen, listening on headphones at my desk job at the Tufts University music library, having spent four years worshipping the Velvet Underground as the greatest band of all time, and ignoring Lou Reed the Solo Artist until now? Why, side one, track one, of course: "Vicious."

Transformer begins in violence. Violence is inflicted upon and then perpetrated by the song's narrator, all while the band deploys an explosive musical violence aimed at the listener. "Vicious," spits Lou 8 seconds into the track, and guitarist/co-producer Mick Ronson answers by slashing through the good-time rock 'n' roll backing with an extra loud, adrenaline-soaked root chord that is one of the most viscerally satisfying guitar parts I know of. Somehow this

---

[1] There are a couple Lou Reed singles that outperformed the track commercially—both "Dirty Blvd." and "What's Good" made #1 on the Billboard Charts much later in Reed's career—but I think it's safe to say that more people remember "Take a Walk on the Wild Side." Wikipedia calls it Lou Reed's "signature song," and though no citation is included for why this is true, it's true.

chord retains its impact as Ronson proceeds to play it after almost every sung line of the song, acting as a sonic exclamation point for a singer who, vocally, ends every line with a period. The lyrics, nakedly expressing violence and hatred, are delivered in a sedated near-monotone, largely empty of affect. The track as a whole is the psychotic lashing out of a man who has been hurt and wants to hurt someone else. Welcome to Lou Reed's most accessible record.

Themes of violence in pop music are not particularly shocking today, nor were they in 1972. But there's something about this violence that is more acutely disturbing than that found in Iggy Pop's Dionysian writhing or Jim Morrison's high poetic drama: it's just so *casual*. "Hey, why don't you swallow razorblades?" Lou suggests, as though asking someone to run down to the corner store and pick up a sixpack for him. He's not just cool; he's ice fucking cold, and he might kill you.

The question posed in *Transformer*'s opening track, and one that remains tantalizingly unanswerable throughout the record, is: Is this guy for real? Is he really this cold and bored, or is he putting it on? What's he hiding? All the glam poses and hip detachment are compelling as theater, but how deep do they run? Has Lou Reed really seen it all, as his songs and general tone as an artist continually suggest?

With regard to his offstage life, we know that Lou certainly "walked the walk"—he was a frequenter of New York's criminalized gay clubs throughout his twenties, he consumed titanic amounts of speed and alcohol, he was into S&M and hung out with transsexuals and got in trouble with authorities. But the difference in asking this kind of question about Lou Reed—the reason that "Are you for real?" remains an unanswerable question—is that Lou Reed never really does try to claim authenticity or sincerity. The whole mystery of *Transformer* and a lot of its magnetic pull is that we can't wonder if he really means it: How can you *mean* emotionlessness, boredom, the very feeling of meaninglessness? Setting himself apart from most singers, who aim to soulfully pour forth with emotion, Lou wants not to mean anything. He performs the rejection of sincerity and the absence of feeling, the message to the world again being: You don't know me, and you never will.

The addictive project for me, then, has been not to interrogate whether or not Reed is being sincere, but to uncover the sincerity in his music that he's trying not to let us see. His performance of cold indifference is, like any instance of punk rock's notorious "fuck off" attitude, the product of deep pain and alienation. Trying to seem devoid of all human content can be more psychologically revealing an act than publicly pouring one's heart out. This is Reed's strategy, and he sticks to it. As he strikingly claimed in a 1972 interview, "I don't have a personality of my own."

I don't believe him for a second. I think he's dropping personal, emotional confessions all over *Transformer*, leaving clues like a criminal at large who secretly wants to be caught. The trick is, they're largely in code. Buried in *Transformer* is a whole diary's worth of emotion from an uncertain, sensitive young man brimming with hurt.

Lou the Queer

Lou Reed is my favorite gay icon. Calling him that is a bit of an awkward fit, since he got married three times (to women) and can be heard on one of his live albums saying, "I'd rather have cancer than be a faggot."

But he's a gay icon nonetheless, and it's his ambivalence and rebelliousness about those kinds of labels that makes him my favorite. Well, that, and the fact that he writes the best songs.

Reed didn't get his first choice: he never had cancer, but he was definitely a faggot. He made that clear to his parents when he was seventeen—although considering how willfully and consistently he aimed to piss off his parents, coming out to them may have been as much motivated by rebelliousness as by honesty. Teenage Lou played loud rock 'n' roll, adopted feminine mannerisms, smoked marijuana, and threw emotional tantrums. This was 1959, and in his middle-class suburban Jewish home, this stuff was way out of bounds.

Though young Lou was clearly having some real difficulties, it was the homosexuality that convinced his doctor that he needed electroshock therapy, and his parents were freaked out enough to force him to go through with it. Eight weeks of brutal treatment changed his life forever. They'd strap him to a table and give him the same dose of voltage as they gave everyone else, regardless of physical size or level of dysfunction. Side effects included confusion and memory loss. As he described it, "You can't read a book because you get to page seventeen and you have to go right back to page one again. Or if you put the book down for an hour and went back to pick up where you started, you didn't remember the pages you read. You had to start all over. If you walked around the block, you forgot where you were."[1] His mind had been fragmented, and some residue of this must have lingered for the rest of his life. He had been a budding fiction writer and aspired to one day author novels. Instead, he'd master and transform the three-minute pop song, condensing and fragmenting his novelistic sensibility into some of the best songs ever written.

Rebellious artist-type or not, if coming out to your parents got you tied to a table and pumped with electricity, you might feel some inner conflict about who you are, or who you should be. You might marry a girl who seemed like someone your parents would approve of. You might say something like "I'd rather have cancer than be a faggot" in public, and not be quite sure if you're being tongue-in-cheek or not.[2]

[1] Victor Bockris, *Transformer: The Lou Reed Story* (London: Vintage, 1995), 14.
[2] A bit of context: this line comes toward the beginning of an epic rambling version of "Walk on the Wild Side" on the 1978 album *Live: Take No Prisoners*, with the band playing but Lou just talking, not ready to sing a full verse. "I have no attitude without a cigarette," he muses. "I'd rather have cancer than be a faggot." Pause. "That wasn't an anti-gay remark. Coming

So anyway. Lou's gay, but not yet an icon, not for a while. He goes to Syracuse University in 1960 to study English, where he has his first affairs with men. He dates women—has a long-term girlfriend for a while who he feels pretty serious about—but has affairs with guys on the side, and he frequents the local gay bar, the Hayloft. In a 1979 issue of *Creem* magazine, Lou talks about his adolescence and early twenties, describing "trying to make yourself feel something toward women when you can't. I couldn't figure out what was wrong. I wanted to fix it up and make it okay. I figured if I sat around and thought about it, I could straighten it out."[3]

He was a ne'er-do-well on campus as much as he had been at his parents' house, taking lots of drugs, drinking too much, and being deliberately provocative to his fellow students. College friend Allan Hyman tells of Lou attending a rush event for Syracuse's Jewish fraternity, Sigma Alpha Mu, purposely looking extremely disheveled, dirty, possibly homeless. Causing a stir of disapproving whispers when he arrived, he proceeded to individually insult everyone

from me it was a compliment." You can't get much more ambiguous and conflicted than that. He says it to piss people off, but then he immediately insists that it's not what it sounds like, and anyway, he's gay so he can say shitty things about gay people. His instinct is to declare himself both gay and superior to gays. He wants the cultural cache that comes with being sexually adventurous as well as the power that comes with being a macho homophobe. Classic bisexual move: trying to have it both ways. (I can say that, by the way, because I'm bisexual. There I go, now I'm doing it too.) Regardless, there's no way it's a compliment, and it lays bare his discomfort with his sexuality and gender.

[3] Bockris, *Transformer*, 49.

in the room, and refused to leave when asked.[4] In short, he was an unusually devoted non-conformist. He was into classic novels, loud guitars, and out-there jazz like Ornette Coleman (he hosted a night-time jazz radio show on campus named "Excursions on a Wobbly Rail," after a Cecil Taylor song, which was soon canceled after complaints about its content[5]). I get the sense that Lou's homosexuality was deeply interwoven with his interest in music and art, as well as his aggressively alienating social presence. Finding himself surrounded by heterosexual jocks and threatened by the social power they held, he became an antagonistic iconoclast to survive. He turned what those around him saw as weaknesses—being gay, feminine, arty, and socially awkward—into weapons, and flaunted them.

All along, he was plotting a fusion of his two main interests: literature and rock 'n' roll. "The songs that became the Velvet Underground songs—you know, I was like, an English major," he recounted in 2009. "So I had had this idea about, you know, write that kind of stuff to a rock song."[6] In his mind, it was an obvious move. "It was such a simple idea, I don't even know if it qualifies as an idea. But that hadn't really existed."[7] Simple, but filtered through his queer, angry

---

[4] Aidan Levy, *Dirty Blvd.: The Life and Music of Lou Reed* (Chicago: Chicago Review Press, 2016), 56.
[5] Levy, *Dirty Blvd.*, 55.
[6] NY Public Library podcast, "Lou Reed on Playing Outside the Box" (New York Public Library, New York, NY, December 8, 2009).
[7] Lou Reed, South by Southwest Music keynote interview (Austin, TX, March 13, 2008).

worldview, that idea became the foundation for something remarkable.

The Velvet Underground formed early in 1965, rehearsing intensively, shuffling the band lineup a bit and getting their first paid gigs late in the year. In December they landed a two-week residency at Cafe Bizarre in Greenwich Village, where they took pride in driving patrons away with their loud dissonant rock 'n' roll accompanied by John Cale's screechy viola. It was here that celebrity visual artist Andy Warhol first saw them, and quickly proposed that they hire him as the band's manager. Warhol was planning to host a nightclub, and he had found the perfect avant-garde band to provide music for these upcoming events. The nightclub concept eventually evolved into a series of events called The Exploding Plastic Inevitable, a multimedia show involving music, screenings of Warhol's films, dance, performance art, and innovative light shows. The Velvet Underground were the house band for these events, held mostly at a rented community hall in New York called the Dom. On the strength of Andy Warhol's well-established name, the shows attracted celebrities, intellectuals, and reporters. If it sounds like a lot of overblown hip spectacle, it was. It was probably easy to miss the fact that this house band was playing almost terrifyingly original music, and was fronted by a truly brilliant songwriter.

Warhol, too, was gay, and his collaborators and employees—referred to collectively as Warhol's superstars—were known for being gay, transgender, kinky, and/or polyamorous. Lou, already a veteran of gay hangouts in New York, felt right at home. "A bunch of us would leave the

Dom really late and go to the after-hours clubs around the Village—Lou knew them all," recalls Andy Warhol.[8] These were good spots for a no-strings-attached sexual rendezvous with a stranger, one of the few pathways to having gay sex in the sixties.

Andy's famous Silver Factory, a headquarters for churning out art and taking in drugs (mostly speed), became a second home to Lou. He became part of a thriving scene and grew fast as a songwriter and musician. This was the freedom he had sought when caged in suburbia and the institutional claustrophobia of Syracuse. It also meant validation as a serious artist, which he'd craved for years, from people with real cultural and intellectual credentials. Warhol was famous, respected, sometimes worshipped, and Lou had his seal of approval.

Lou had sexual dalliances with men from the Factory. He and Billy Name, an artist and lighting designer who was responsible for decking out the Factory in its iconic tinfoil design, connected deeply and enjoyed an off-and-on love affair in the late sixties. But he was also having an affair with his college girlfriend Shelley Albin again, who by now was married to another man. It was an emotionally fraught situation that you can hear about in the Velvet Underground's "Pale Blue Eyes" ("The fact that you are married / Only proves you're my best friend / But it's truly truly a sin"). Albin refused to divorce her husband and eventually cut Lou out of her life.

[8]Bockris, *Transformer*, 126.

I'm compelled by the tug-of-war going on here, between the underground artsy lifestyle and the middle-class normalcy Reed's parents hoped he would find his way back to. It was also, I hardly need to point out, a battle between homo- and heterosexuality. I don't mean to suggest that Lou Reed felt guilty about his sexual relationships with other men or his betrayal of his parents' hopes for him. But the freedom and instability of a life in art can compound the instability that comes with a rejection of the sexual behaviors the square world demands of us queers at every turn. We all know how much easier and less problematic it can seem to be heterosexual, and many of us achingly ask ourselves in dark moments if we wouldn't be better off learning how to fake our way through an institutionally sanctioned life as a straight cis-gendered Normal Person. If these thoughts still haunt the troubled queer in the twenty-first century, one can imagine how powerful a sway they must have held over a broke, uncertain twenty-something in the sixties. On a bad week, anyway.

Here, read this passage from an interview with Lou Reed:

> We were living together in a thirty-dollar-a-month apartment and we really didn't have any money. We used to eat oatmeal all day and all night and give blood among other things, or pose for these nickel or fifteen-cent tabloids they have every week. And when I posed for them my picture came out and it said I was a sex-maniac killer and that I had killed fourteen children and had tape-recorded it and played it in a barn in Kansas at midnight. And when John's picture came out in the paper, it said he

had killed his lover because his lover was going to marry his sister, and he didn't want his sister to marry a fag.[9]

Can you feel the intensity of the simultaneously thrilling and exhausting position these young men are in? Can you feel the penetratingly disgusted and fetishizing gaze of the mainstream? Can you feel the pressure to go home and work in the family business and marry the girl next door, and the pure electricity of refusing to do so?

Thus, the charged, overwhelming power of the Velvet Underground.

* * *

To be clear: homosexuality in the mid-sixties was not okay, as far as the wider culture was concerned. Most people saw it as a menace and a sign of moral decay. The socially conservative backlash to gay activity in New York City in particular was quite violent. In preparation for the 1964 World's Fair, Mayor Robert Wagner launched a campaign to "clean up the city," which in part meant closing down as many gay bars as possible. The NYPD used undercover cops to illegally entrap homosexuals and then arrest them, and the cops would stage violent raids of bars known for gay activity. Nor was this animosity limited to police. To give you an idea of the general feeling toward queers: after the Fawn, a gay dance bar in Greenwich Village was closed down early in 1964, the *New York Times* ran a front page story headlined, "Growth of Overt Homosexuality in City Provokes Wide Concern."

[9]Bockris, *Transformer*, 88.

But gay bars were habitually raided by cops every once in a while for many years before that, and the brutal pattern continued for many years afterward. London-based Tom Robinson's masterful protest song "Glad to Be Gay," released in 1978, offers a picture of what was going on even in the seventies, telling how police were "raiding our pubs for no reason at all / Lining the customers up by the wall / Picking out people and knocking them down / Resisting arrest as they're kicked on the ground / Searching their houses and calling them queer." Yet, in the anthemic minor key singalong, Robinson repeatedly insists that he's "glad to be gay . . . happy that way." It's a beleaguered but exultant sentiment that brilliantly captures the mood of a generation of people struggling to be out of the closet in a society deeply unfriendly to them. As strong as the pull is to closet oneself and avoid homophobic violence, the triumph is being able to affirm one's identity in the face of an onslaught of discouragement.

Lou Reed, despite the support he had from so many like-minded queers, would often teeter on the edge of giving up the outlaw life and going back to the life sanctioned by the straight world he'd left behind. He would step back and forth across the line that separated the freaks from the squares, defying people's expectations on both sides of it. Eventually he would succeed in destroying that line, at least in his own life, altogether.

* * *

Like so many marginalized populations, queers spent the sixties getting increasingly intolerant of the abuses they suffered at the hands of the mainstream. In 1965, Dick Leitsch, president of the New York Mattachine Society—a branch of one of the earliest gay rights advocacy groups, first founded in Los Angeles in 1950—advocated direct confrontation of the authorities in the form of public gay protests. At Leitsch's urging, pro-gay activists marched on the White House and the United Nations that April. Homosexual visibility and insurgency in America increased and intensified from that point on, and by the summer of 1969 it reached a pitch that inaugurated gay liberation as a nationally recognized human rights movement.

In the early morning hours of June 28, 1969, a routinely vicious raid of a popular gay and transgender bar, the Stonewall Inn, turned into the historic Stonewall riots when the 200+ bar patrons fought back. Various arrested individuals refused to go with the police; when officers began handcuffing people, sometimes striking them, knocking them down and/or throwing them into police vans, the crowd turned into a violent mob. Homeless people and patrons of neighboring bars saw the commotion and joined in, throwing coins, cans, bottles, and bricks at the police. The violence lasted for days and the conversation around gay resistance became ubiquitous and radicalized. The formation of the Gay Liberation Front and the Gay Activist Alliance followed soon after those riots.

Suddenly, a revolution was underway. These activist groups and others became known for their "zaps," public protests disrupting the usual business of civic life demanding legislation to end housing and job discrimination against homosexuals. Marches for gay rights became a regular occurrence in New York, such as the first gay pride parades, held in New York on June 28, 1970—the first anniversary of the Stonewall raid. ("Out of the closets, into the streets!" went one of the chanted slogans, which Lou Reed would adapt for his song "Make Up.") In December 1971, *Life* magazine ran an 11-page photo essay called *Homosexuals in Revolt*. "They resent what they consider to be savage discrimination," it read. "Never before have homosexuals been so visible."[10]

Widespread homophobia in American culture notwithstanding, there were certainly strands of pop culture that reflected the rise of gay visibility. *The Boys in the Band* (1968) was a massively successful off-Broadway play that sympathetically portrayed a group of troubled gay men; it ran for more than 1,000 performances and was made into a hit movie in 1970. In 1969, *Midnight Cowboy* featured the first onscreen sexual encounter between two men in a nonporn film, and won multiple Academy Awards, including Best Picture. The Kinks had a no. 2 hit on the British pop charts with the risqué "Lola" in 1970, with lyrics like "Girls will be boys and boys will be girls" and "I'm glad I'm a man and so is Lola." In the United States the song stayed in the Billboard Top 40 for twelve weeks. And then there was David Bowie, declaring "I'm gay, and always have been" in *Melody Maker* as his exposure grew by leaps and bounds—but we'll save him for later.

These seismic social developments set the foundation for new cultural conditions, in which Lou Reed would be able to find his first commercial success by dipping into

[10]Jeremy Reed, *Waiting For The Man: The Life and Music of Lou Reed* (London: Omnibus Press, 2014), 56.

glam rock signifiers and marketing his androgyny and non-heterosexuality as edgy and cool. Such a move would have been impossible a few years earlier. One might argue that what really made the difference between the Velvet Underground's extreme lack of record sales and Lou Reed's solo success was that the Velvets came before America recognized a gay rights revolution in progress, whereas *Transformer* came after. Between the release of "Sister Ray" and "Walk on the Wild Side," the idea of an openly gay lead singer had shifted, as far as the mainstream music scene was concerned, from career-killing embarrassment to marketable selling point. Thanks in large part to the gay rights movement, Lou's queerness had become his secret weapon.

Lou the Failure

If I'm going to be really pants-down honest here, I have to admit that I take pleasure in watching Lou Reed wriggle and suffer in his late twenties and early thirties in a way that is downright sadistic.

I'm a singer, songwriter, and bandleader myself, deeply influenced (if it's not obvious by now) by Lou Reed. As my own twenties went on, and as each successive album I labored over and released yielded incrementally increasing public attention and exponentially greater personal disappointment, I started to get worried that my life as an artist wasn't going to work out. I began to take comfort in reading Wikipedia bios of successful artists who had taken until their thirties to find the critical acclaim and financial dividends that allowed them to continue making art full-time. People like Leonard Cohen, who released his first record when he was thirty-three (I was willing to ignore his considerable success as a poet and novelist in his twenties), Tom Waits, who didn't really hit his artistic or commercial stride until a decade into his career, and the brilliant late-blooming filmmaker Errol Morris—these stories were a soothing balm to my anxious twenty-seven-year-old mind.

Be patient, this carefully curated, selectively blind list of slow burners assured me. *Your time is just around the corner.*

I'm writing as if I've stopped doing this, but truthfully, it's an ongoing situation. I'm still hungrily devouring these bios hoping that my own will look the same before too long.

The thing that's either sad or, if you're a frustrated artist like myself, perhaps sadistically satisfying about Lou Reed is that he actually desperately wanted, from the very beginning, to be a huge success. My guess is that most fans of the Velvet Underground don't realize this, being that the band is so often celebrated for its pure refusal to compromise, its continual willingness to record music a million miles away from something that could be played on commercial radio in the mid-to-late sixties, and the presence of the word "underground" in its name. But they were in fact very hungry for commercial success. At the same time, they were hungry for avant-garde credentials, which proved more readily available to folks like them. After all, Andy Warhol chose them as his house band—it makes sense that they presented themselves as equal parts confrontational art and mass market-ready consumer good. It's uncanny how perfectly matched Warhol and Reed were as artists: gay amphetamine users who believed in pop culture as the perfect avenue for their twisted brand of high art.

But the Velvet Underground were not a huge success, at least not while the band were together. They were sort of flirting with and on the brink of a potential commercial breakthrough in 1970, which is of course when Lou Reed perversely decided he couldn't take it anymore and left. The story of his departure from the band is not widely known—which is surprising because it's such a good story, but also unsurprising because it makes Reed look so deeply uncool. Just the type of anecdote he might prefer to gloss over.

It goes like this: in the summer of 1970, the Velvet Underground had a six-week residency at Max's Kansas City, and Lou Reed was suffocating. Though Max's had been a favorite hangout of his for years, he hated playing there that summer, having become increasingly ambivalent about the band's direction. Yet, a buzz was at last starting to legitimately build around the Velvet Underground, and their new album *Loaded*, designed as a pop smash with big hit singles, was nearly finished. Steve Sesnick, their manager since they cut ties with Andy Warhol, was convinced they could be as big as the Rolling Stones, and the band, despite themselves, was being infected by this optimism. Like Warhol, Reed felt that Art could be treated as a capitalist enterprise, and capitalist enterprises as Art. It was natural for him to consider fame the logical next step. But he was characteristically conflicted about this, too, and the effort to please a mainstream audience (one that was still largely hypothetical) soon began to wear him down.

Sesnick had also taken a new approach to managing the band's image, which was to emphasize bassist Doug Yule as the star and let the less-conventionally charismatic Lou Reed fade into the background despite his position as band founder and main songwriter. As a result, Reed began to fight for dominance in the band, at times by imitating Doug Yule's onstage persona and trying out bombastic dance moves onstage rather than sticking to his dramatic stock-still couldn't-care-less pose. This toxic dynamic, plus a punishing touring schedule and a regular diet of amphetamines, pushed Reed to a breaking point. It all added up to a sense of total alienation from his job: "I never in my life thought I would not do what I believed in and there I was, not doing what I believed in, that's all, and it made me sick."[1]

August 23, 1970, Lou showed up to Max's having firmly decided that this was his last performance with the band, but not having told anyone. Shortly before the show, he confided in original VU drummer Mo Tucker, who was on a leave of absence from the band because she was pregnant, letting her know that he was quitting. She tried to talk him out of it, but he told her his mind was made up. He had been reduced from the band's driving creative force to its ineffectual, insincere frontispiece. He was leaving, against all social and career momentum, no matter how unplanned his future, no matter how much he had depended on the identity and status the band gave him.

Warhol associate Brigid Polk was in the habit of recording shows she attended on a portable cassette machine, and the recording of the Velvet Underground released in 1972 as *Live at Max's Kansas City* is believed to have been from this performance. If it was, what we have is a recording of a band who, apart from the lead singer, were unaware that they were playing their final concert. Via Polk's single mono microphone, we hear a raw document of Lou Reed songs adapted to the style of the more successful rock bands of the

[1]Bockris, *Transformer*, 175.

era. The Velvet Underground was plainly aiming to sound more like the Who or Cream, with new drummer Billy Yule (Doug's brother) adding bombastic drum fills and Sterling Morrison leaning into a bluesy guitar-hero style that had been anathema to the band a few years ago. Still, the songs are great, and if you like late-sixties rock 'n' roll, they're doing it really well, having toured the hell out of these songs. Lou sounds cool but engaged, often getting audibly caught up in the band's manic energy. He once said that this show was the only one of that summer he enjoyed, because he knew it was all over after that evening.

The kicker is that after the show, Lou's parents showed up to drive him to his childhood home in Long Island, where he would move in with them now that his music career was over. He introduced them to Sterling Morrison for the first time—a bewildering surprise to Morrison, since Reed had for years been referencing the looming threat that his parents would one day show up and cart him off to the loony bin. Then he told manager Steve Sesnick that he was leaving the band, got into his parents' car and went home with them, like a teenager at the end of a high school dance. In the next months he took a job as a typist at his father's accounting firm for $40 a week.

Try to feel the total perverse desperation of this move, its perfect dichotomous symbolism, its enormous cowardice and simultaneous bravery. Though not a public moment—in fact, the heralding of an end to public moments for Lou for a while—it was a performance as evocative and charged as any in his career up to that point, the audience being his band, his parents and, most importantly, himself. Max's was the geographic locus of Lou Reed's identity as New York underground scenester, with its famous back room full of drug use and sexual advances and hip artists self-consciously provoking one another. It was the room where his self-made character, designed to be as far away from his middle-class suburban origins as imaginable, was allowed full realization and free rein. Directly from this room he returns to his parents' house, the opposite end of his world, and a place where his new druggy promiscuous artist identity had no meaning or power.

There's a kind of despair to this moment, an admission of defeat as someone who tried to be a rebel and failed. But there's also a bold defiance of its own kind. Imagine the courage it took, after more than five years of exhausting and life-encompassing effort poured into this band, with scores of others becoming increasingly excited about the group's momentum, to recognize that the project had become a betrayal of its own ideals and walk away from all of it. To turn your back on a world of friends, collaborators, and associates and choose a life diametrically opposed to the culture you've been living and breathing. It's a crazy thing to do, and must have taken great willpower.

This is how Lou Reed meets failure, how the leader of the one of the greatest bands ever bows out: in a blaze of glory and shame utterly, ambiguously mingled. At this pivotal moment in his career, our rebellious rock 'n' roll hero rebels totally against the very concept of rebellion he began with, which has been commodified and turned into a parody of itself. He saw himself, as he would again and again, turning into a cartoon, a predetermined character, lifeless and trapped. The only way forward was to proceed circularly all the way back to his beginning: Long Island, under his parents' authority, no idea who he might become.

* * *

This identity crisis was not anomalous in Reed's biography; far from it. He would continue to create selves that he would grow to hate and eventually jettison, he would repeatedly draw near to lasting, full-fledged success and then spit on everyone who thought he might finally have been about to succeed. Look at him wriggling through the seventies: he achieves real superstardom with *Transformer* and responds by making *Berlin* in 1973, a desperately bleak novelistic approach to a concept album with nary a single on it. When the public fails to respond with the same enthusiasm they had for the pop-friendly *Transformer*, he fires back with *Sally Can't Dance*, a rather soulless radio-ready sell-out that outperforms any of his previous albums on the charts. Next, in case you were enjoying yourself, comes *Metal Machine Music*, a four-sided songless noise feast that is so legendarily unpleasant that it's hard to believe any record label would allow it to be released in 1975. Which of course he follows with *Coney Island Baby*, basically a collection of polished love songs (though punctuated halfway through by "Kicks," a horrifying song about murdering people for sexual pleasure). And on and on through the whole of his career. The last two albums he released were a collection of ambient music to accompany the practice of T'ai Chi (*Hudson River Wind Meditations*, 2007) and a beguiling, wildly unpopular collaboration with Metallica (*Lulu*, 2011)—output no one expected or asked for.

One might think Reed is merely being deliberately contrarian, reveling in his unpredictability, and one would be half right. That Lou Reed's discography is basically a collection of symptoms of Oppositional Defiance Disorder is one of the pleasures and frustrations of listening to his work. But there's more than that. Lou knows there's no success like failure, and that failure's no success at all. As with Bob Dylan, the need for fame, success, and admiration battle with disdain for and alienation from the public. The equilibrium between these two impulses, messily achieved over time, is what makes the artist—Dylan or Reed—unforgettable, both as a pop star and as a difficult genius, both the friend and enemy of his own audience.

There are a number of artists who embody this dynamic as public figures. One thing that may be unique to Lou is that I think this is happening for him on a private level as well. The conflict between artifice and authenticity goes deep into his identity, as it does for a lot of queers. He performs identities and then gives them up as he fails in his ability to fully inhabit them. He becomes a heroin user and defines himself as such in front of everybody for the rest of his career—"it's my life, and it's my wife," over and over again for decades—but he actually kicked heroin pretty quickly, much preferring amphetamines. He becomes a pioneering avant-garde proto-noise musician with John Cale in the Velvet Underground and then turns around and kicks Cale out of the band to write sweet quiet pop songs and attempts at hit singles. He writes an album "loaded with hits" and then quits his band before its release, quits music entirely for a year and a half. He's a gay drug addict artist for years and then he goes home to work for his father and weds a suburban Jewish girl (the marriage doesn't last). And of course, he makes *Transformer*, at last his huge hit record with a very on-trend glam image to match, then rejects the whole conceit, and denigrates glam rock as a "faggot junkie trip." His life is a string of failures to live up to the identities he takes on.

His problem, or his gift, is that no self that his audience can digest fits him comfortably, and he always ends up tearing the latest self violently off like a too-small suit on a hot afternoon. He's never really felt comfortable his whole life, since like so many non-heterosexuals he spent his youth presenting an idealized self to the world that was a betrayal of the taboo truth. When he did try, messily, to come out of the closet and declare some kind of authentic self to those close to him, he got high-voltage fried by adults who found the real Lou unacceptable.

His career compels me most of all because of how it acts out his and my own bitter struggle between whether to be someone who the world can accept and love—whoever that might be—or whether to be myself—whoever that might be. We search desperately for someone to be, for a life that might be livable, for a self that might be real. Ultimately, the search is wrong-headed and doomed from the start. Looking for the easy solution of a ready-made way to be, we find only characters that don't ring true, poses we can't hold for long. Our true authenticity, in fact, saturates the struggle; it is the search itself. I propose that for folks like me and Lou, the real meaning of queerness is defined by continual transformation, being permanently on the run from the straight authorities (real, imagined or both) that would try to force us to be something untrue.

And then eventually, maybe, you grow older and stop worrying so much about it. I don't know yet; I'm only thirty. The same age, by the way, that Lou Reed was when he recorded *Transformer*. And now perhaps my authoring a book about this particular album at this particular time is starting to make a kind of sense.

Lou and Bowie

Transformer was the explosive collision of two ascendant satellites, Lou Reed and David Bowie, resulting in a light in the sky brighter than either of them would have been on their own. It was a perfect collaboration perfectly timed, and never to be repeated. How and why did it happen, and why was it so fleeting?

The answer to that question begins in 1966, shortly after David had changed his surname from Jones to Bowie, when he was forming and quitting a series of bands in search of a habitable public identity. His manager had been to the United States and attained a test pressing of the Velvet Underground's yet-to-be-released debut record, which he gave to Bowie. Bowie's mind was blown. His then-band the Riot Squad covered "Waiting for the Man" immediately and also recorded a bizarre song called "Little Toy Soldier" that shamelessly plagiarizes a chunk of "Venus in Furs." He wasn't sure yet what he was going to do with this new influence, but the VU was, for him, an attitudinal game-changer. "Everything I both felt and didn't know about rock music was opened to me on one unreleased disc," he wrote in 2003. "With the opening throbbing, sarcastic bass and guitar of

'I'm Waiting for the Man,' the linchpin, the keystone of my ambition was driven home. . . . I was hearing a degree of cool that I had no idea was humanly sustainable."[1]

In the years to follow, Bowie would incorporate what excited him about the Velvet Underground into his own aesthetic revision of the archetypal rock star. Androgyny, street-smart toughness, and hard drugs were all repurposed to make David Bowie into a fascinating character that pop culture had never quite seen before.

By the summer of 1971, that character was fully formed, but not yet fully recognized as the phenomenon he would become. *Hunky Dory*, a breakthrough album for Bowie creatively but not a commercial success, was finished but yet to be released. First, Bowie needed a new record deal. He came to New York City in August to sign a contract with RCA recordings, the label he would stay with for the next decade.

In the meantime, withdrawn from the music scene and living with his parents on Long Island, Lou Reed had been getting restless. Amid frequent trips to the city to spend time with his new fiancée, Bettye, Lou befriended Richard and Lisa Robinson, bohemian scenesters and music business professionals who hosted many a wild party. Richard was an A&R man for RCA,[2] which meant that it was his job to find the next burgeoning underground phenomenon and sign them to the label. Lou Reed—the local legend who

---

[1] David Bowie, "Bowie Rules NYC," *New York Magazine*, September 18, 2003.
[2] Artists & Repertoire. A record label's talent scout and liaison between artist and label.

never broke through—was an obvious choice, and the new acquaintances began plotting his solo career. He had, of course, never stopped writing songs, and he would debut new compositions at gatherings in the Robinsons' living room, playing solo on an acoustic guitar.

As Reed and Bowie signed to RCA nearly simultaneously, a meeting was arranged. Bowie wanted to meet his hero, and Lou had heard a lot of buzz about Bowie—maybe this stylish, androgynous twenty-four-year-old was someone it could be useful to know. The two of them, accompanied by some eager RCA employees, various friends, and Bowie's manager, went out to dinner, sizing each other up. Each had something the other wanted, though it wasn't yet clear what. Over the course of the next year and a half, each artist would use the other as a stepping stone to the fame and fortune of which both had dreamed.

* * *

It appears that as much as David Bowie was ready for rock stardom, rock stardom was ready for David Bowie. In retrospect, the concept of a singular rock 'n' roll hero seems to have been left wide open and specially prepared for his arrival.

In the mid-sixties rock music had rapidly, shockingly developed sharp fangs with which to tear at the flesh of the conservative establishment. Chart-topping hit songs were the flags waving at the head of a cluster of cultural movements that were briefly able to see themselves as part of a unified trend. But by the early seventies, what was vital and dangerous about hip music and hippie culture had been neutralized and repackaged into a marketable, one-big-happy-family message. Feel-good tunes by Three Dog Night, Chicago, and James Taylor topped the charts and sapped them of their political energy.[3]

The rock genre's identity was increasingly disintegrating, with the break-up of the Beatles, the absence or obsolescence of Bob Dylan, and increasingly bloated incarnations of heroes like the Rolling Stones and the Who. We get an unmistakable sign of how people are starting to view pop music when Don McLean has a smash hit with "American Pie," a self-important epic bemoaning the death of music, nostalgic for the two-minute shots of adrenaline with which Buddy Holly and other early rock 'n' rollers had injected the culture a decade and a half previous. (And what did a founding elder statesman like Chuck Berry have to say at a time like this? Why, "My Ding-a-Ling," a childish and regrettable novelty hit.)

Thus, the music scene is primed for something new. No one wants to watch rock fizzle out like this; it's just a matter of who's going to come to fill the gap. Enter David Bowie, T. Rex, and glam rock: musical saviors from an alternate universe. The scene needs a good kick in the ass, and Bowie, in a very self-aware and intentional way, delivers it with a "wham, bam, thank you ma'am." Bowie's first really big splash is the release of the 7" single *Starman / Suffragette City* in April 1972, a

---

[3] I find Three Dog Night particularly depressing. While they essentially encouraged their fans to be drugged-out, passive children in songs like "Joy to the World" and "Black and White," Richard Nixon was being reelected president of the United States in a landslide victory.

Top Ten hit in the UK. In June, Bowie releases his stunning dystopian concept album *The Rise and Fall of Ziggy Stardust and the Spiders from Mars* and performs "Starman" on Top of the Pops in July. Soon, a parade of bands marketed as glam or glitter rock, some exciting and some embarrassing, marches across the pop charts: Roxy Music, the New York Dolls, the Sweet, and Gary Glitter are all enabled to make their mark in Bowie's wake. The game, for better or for worse, has been changed, and Bowie is its new messiah.

But he knows that, more than anyone else's, it was Lou Reed's creative influence that got him there. So he covers Velvet Underground songs and drops Lou's name constantly, which, as a bonus, lends him a lot of helpful street cred. "Some V.U., White Light returned with thanks," you can read on the back of the *Hunky Dory* LP sleeve, written next to the title of the Velvets-esque "Queen Bitch." One outtake from the *Ziggy Stardust* album was called "Velvet Goldmine."

In the throes of this rise to power, it must have been weighed heavily on Bowie to watch Lou Reed release his eponymous solo debut, produced by Richard Robinson, to widespread apathy in April 1972. Considered a disappointment by many contemporary fans and certainly by RCA, *Lou Reed* is an underwhelming inaugural statement. It's mostly made up of rejected Velvet Underground songs, but played by a crack team of polished professional studio musicians, including members of Elton John's band and the progressive rock group Yes. The album is so eager to sound like the radio airplay of its time that "Walk and Talk It" begins with a direct quote of the opening riff from the Rolling Stones hit single "Brown

Sugar." Looking back, it's not exactly what one would hope for from the godfather of punk.

If you ask me, Lou was trying to play the game. He wanted success, not the aggressive amateur approach of the failed Velvet Underground, so he worked with highly professional people who made hit records. Bowie, however, knows Lou deserves better—or anyway, *cooler*. Almost the first thing Bowie does with his international stardom is propose that he and his bandmate Mick Ronson produce the next Lou Reed record, and get it right this time.

* * *

A transformer is a device that adapts voltage, allowing an electrical appliance (for example, a guitar amplifier) of one level of voltage to be used with a device of a different voltage. When a band using American equipment goes to play rock 'n' roll in England, they need a transformer. It brings one kind of energy into another context. Vinny LaPorta, the then-teenaged guitar player Lou recruited to tour his solo debut, recalls a possible genesis of the follow-up album's title: "We were at a diner, just eating and waiting, because we had our amplifiers from America and we needed these transformers. . . . We kept goofing, going, 'What are we waiting for? The transformer people! We can't play until they get here. It's the transformer people.' I think that's how Lou got the name of the album."[4]

The metaphor is certainly apt for what Reed and Bowie are trying to do here. Lou Reed carries with him a certain kind of

---

[4] Levy, *Dirty Blvd.*, 191.

energy that, up until this album, has never successfully been amplified in a mainstream pop context. It's as though his enormous power as an artist and performer has fried every circuit he's tried to send it through, getting him dropped from labels, fired from gigs, and ignored by the wider public. What he needs is a voltage adapter: something to harness his gift and make it usable, to amplify it in a sustainable way. This is the album's goal, and in terms of accessibility and profitability, it succeeds. The question is whether this pop adaptation of Lou Reed is faithful to his real strengths or disappointingly neutralizes his impact.

At the end of Reed's tour of the UK supporting his debut, the band went home to New York, but Lou Reed went to London to record. *Transformer* was recorded over ten days in August 1972, about six hours a day, at Trident Studios.[5] The choice of musicians hired to play on the album may have been influenced by Reed and Bowie's shared love of jazz: drummer John Halsey was in the jazz-rock group Patto, while bassist/tubaist Herbie Flowers, a member of the bands Blue Mink and CCS, considered himself a jazz musician first, rock musician second. And Bowie recruited Ronnie Ross, his childhood saxophone teacher, to play sax on "Walk on the Wild Side" and "Goodnight Ladies."

Offbeat jazz-inflected elements aside, the main idea here was to make a powerful rock record, full of both Lou Reed's sexually deviant fuck-you attitude and accessible and memorable pop hooks. Most of the album sounds like it could have been outtakes from *Hunky Dory* or *Ziggy*

[5]Ibid., 193.

Stardust, only with a different lead singer. Crunchy rhythm guitar, dramatic drum fills, and the maudlin piano balladry of "Perfect Day" (a track much in the mode of Bowie's "Life on Mars") combine to unmistakably mark the album as a Bowie production. Which raises the question, how much control did Lou have over this project, and how much has he ceded his aesthetics to his new creative partner?

In the film *Almost Famous* (2000), set in 1973, notorious music writer Lester Bangs (played by Philip Seymour Hoffman) asks the budding teenage journalist William Miller (Patrick Fugit) if he likes Lou Reed. Miller responds, "The early stuff. In his new stuff he's trying to be Bowie. He should just be himself." Bangs—who in real life was one of Lou's biggest admirers and most lovingly harsh critics—answers wryly, "Yeah, but if Bowie's doin' Lou, and Lou's doin' Bowie—Lou's still doin' Lou."

I'm on board with this statement—almost. It's true that Bowie's doin' Lou, and Lou's doin' Bowie, but does that indeed mean Lou is still doin' Lou? I see *Transformer* as Lou aping Bowie's bastardized version of Lou—doing an impression of an impression of himself. The Velvet Underground never actually sounded like the *Transformer* versions of "Andy's Chest" or "Satellite of Love," with their kitschy backup vocals and lumbering rhythm section. Lou's been filtered through Bowie and his Spiders from Mars over the course of a few years and now is not quite recognizable to himself. Which is not to say he won't go along with it. He doesn't really know what he wants his records to sound like anymore, anyway. Still in the artistic crisis that led him to leave the Velvet Underground, he's glad to let his biggest fan, a manic, newly famous Englishman, take his sedated hand and tell him what Lou Reed is supposed to sound like. At least *somebody* knows the answer to that question.

What they come up with feels both authentic and false, the work of an artist whose perspective has been purposely twisted into something more marketable. No accident there: "I wanted to get popular, so I could be the biggest schlock around," Reed said in 1973. "And I turned out really big schlock, because my shit's better than other people's diamonds."[6] This statement is likely a deliberately perverse baiting of an interviewer, but I don't doubt that there's a kernel of truth to it. *Transformer* was a sell-out, jumping on the trendiest bandwagon of the moment: glam rock. It just also happens to be really good. Lou is shrewdly exploiting Bowie as much as Bowie is Lou, and in the process, because they're both so good at making rock 'n' roll, they're producing a classic.

RCA Records made a radio spot for the release of *Transformer* that may have been amusing, disturbing or both to Reed. Over a medley of the most hard-rocking moments of the album, the announcer reads: "In the midst of all the make-believe madness, the mock depravity and the pseudo-sexual anarchists, Lou Reed is the real thing. Lou Reed: the original. He's been one since the birth of the New York underground, and now he's back with a new album: Transformer."

So Reed is advertised as honest, as opposed to all the phonies.[7] In the process of capitalizing on his "real"-ness, he

---

[6] Bockris, *Transformer*.
[7] I'm very curious about what a "psuedo-sexual anarchist" is—unless they're talking about David Bowie? And when was "the birth of the New York

reaches an apex of phoniness which he will never match in all his career. Bowie, whether to his credit or discredit, took him there.

Together, they present an alternative to the future of rock music a million miles away from the likes of Three Dog Night. As music critic Ken Tucker put it: "In the face of the hippie era's sincerity, intimacy and generosity, Bowie presented irony, distance and self-absorption." In an era where nobody trusts anyone they hear on the radio or see on TV, it was refreshing to find someone who wasn't pretending to be just like the regular folks in the audience.

Throughout his career Bowie aims to create distance between himself and his work, between himself and his audience. This is an aspect he noticed immediately in the Velvet Underground, and part of what made hearing them such a sea change moment for him. "The music [on *The Velvet Underground & Nico*] was savagely indifferent to my feelings," he wrote. "It didn't care if I liked it or not. It could give a fuck."[8] But this distance from and indifference to the audience, which came so naturally to Lou Reed, became, in Bowie's hands, a gateway to a pure artifice that had nothing to do with the Velvet Underground's plainspoken, tough prose-poetry. Bowie wanted distance so he could create a fantasy, an artificial icon with the power to transfigure culture and make it less boring. Lou's version of distance from the audience is understatement and lack of affect

---

underground?" Does he mean the Velvet Underground? Does it matter?
[8] Bowie, "Bowie Rules NYC."

while he tells, essentially, the truth about himself and the world around him. Where Bowie wants to create his own dystopian world, Reed wants to shine a light on the dark places of the real one.

One might agree with what the RCA radio ad suggests: Bowie is a phony and Reed is authentic. This would be to overlook Reed's dodgy, noncommittal career path as well as Bowie's stunning moments of earned emotional sincerity. But if Bowie is one of the "pseudo-sexual anarchists" and Reed is "the real thing," keep in mind that that doesn't necessarily tell you which one of them makes better records.

This core difference between the two artists is thrown into stark relief when questions of queerness come up. Here's David Bowie talking to NPR's Terry Gross in 2002:

> GROSS: So did you see the kind of gender aspects of your performance, you know, dressing—you know, sometimes wearing an evening gown, sometimes, you know—often wearing lipstick, dyeing your hair, lots of eye makeup. Did you see the gender stuff as being a statement about postmodernism or a statement about sexuality?
> BOWIE: Well, neither—I think they were just devices to create this new distancing from the subject matter.

Bowie, as he has confessed more explicitly elsewhere, was faking his bisexuality and gender ambiguity.[9] Reed was not.

---

[9] "I didn't ever feel that I was a real bisexual. It was like I was making all the moves, down to the situation of actually trying it out with some guys. But for me, I was more magnetized by the whole gay scene, which was

But as for showy femininity—makeup, glitter, etc.—that was pretty much a stage persona for both artists, one which, for Lou, clearly didn't stick. A year later he's looking pretty much masculine again, as he did in the sixties. He didn't need a device to create distance. For one thing, sounding (and being) emotionally distant is his specialty; for another, his artistic goal is honesty, not artifice. In many ways, Lou Reed is fighting *against* his automatic tendency to dissemble. Most of his career is a quest to write a straightforward, three-chord song that tells the plain truth. And for that kind of an artist, Bowie's theatrical version of rock is an uncomfortable fit.

The Bowie superstar machine took Lou Reed and made him into an icon, amplifying and distorting him. What became famous was a stylized snapshot of Lou, not the man himself. It becomes almost impossible to pin down who the real Lou Reed is because, at least on *Transformer*, he's not cast as himself. He's cast to play the pop culture version of himself, the Lou Reed his fans have imagined was behind his earlier records.

Admittedly, this is part of what celebrity is: turning a person into a symbol. Both Bowie and Reed appreciate this kind of iconography; after all, they're both admirers of Andy Warhol. "I'd like to be a gallery / put you all inside my show," Bowie sings in "Andy Warhol" (1971). "Andy Warhol looks a

---

underground. . . . It was like another world that I really wanted to buy into. So I made efforts to go and get into it. . . . The irony of it was that I was not gay. I was physical about it, but frankly it wasn't enjoyable." *Bowie on Bowie: Interviews and Encounters with David Bowie*, ed. Sean Egan (Chicago Review Press, 2015), 246–47.

scream / Hang him on my wall." To Bowie, Warhol represents the dehumanization of the artist into art piece, into celebrity icon. Warhol repurposed and distorted Elvis Presley and Marilyn Monroe into his material; Bowie used Andy Warhol, Iggy Pop, and Lou Reed.

Lou Reed, of course, was an eager collaborator in this move, but dropped hints all along that he was conflicted about it, even in the songs themselves. If the album seems uneven or half-hearted, this is why: because the singer, watching himself move further than ever before into the artifice of celebrity, is not entirely sure he even wants to go through with it.

After *Transformer*, Reed is left with the fallout of becoming a rock 'n' roll symbol along with the dividends. He will be rich and famous. But he'll also be plagued for the rest of his career by nosy and tone-deaf journalists, moronic fans, cheap imitators, and the impossible task of managing how the pop culture world sees him. "Watch me turn into Lou Reed before your very eyes!" he mocks on the epic rambling version of "Walk on the Wild Side" from 1978's *Live: Take No Prisoners*. "I do Lou Reed better than anybody so I thought I'd get in on it." It's the sound of an artist alienated from his famous persona and its uncontrollable mutations in a scene and ascendant genre he influenced more than anyone—and thus, one he can't resist getting in on. Again he's doing an imitation of an imitation of himself. But the real thing, in fleeting moments, still shines through.

Side One

Side One

"Vicious"
Lou and Hate

Leadoff tracks are important, especially at a moment in one's career when the audience is unsure what to expect, if anything, from an artist. If Lou's previous eponymous album felt a little unfocused and tepid, disappointing to fans of the sonically aggressive approach of the Velvet Underground, then here is a song that does what many at the time thought Lou Reed was supposed to do: *rock*. (Albeit a pretty sanitized and conventional approach compared to that of, say, "Sister Ray.") That, clearly, is the most basic intention of this song: just to be loud and brash and tough and cool. But, as in pretty much every Lou Reed song, there are secrets and ambiguities. There's something going on below the surface, and once you've started singing along with this catchy number, you begin to notice some uncomfortable things about what you're singing.

To open *Transformer*, Lou Reed spits out an insult, calls someone a name—"vicious"—and then immediately subverts that insult. "You hit me with a flower." A word whose meaning seemed so clear is complicated by the ensuing phrase. Is our hard-rocking tough guy confessing weakness, admitting vulnerability to the power of a limp petunia? Or is he being sarcastic, saying, "your attempts to hurt me bounce off, they mean nothing to me," an ironic putdown? Either way, the effect is to mess with our image of toughness. The band does everything it can to sonically associate itself with rock masculinity. And the singer grunts out lyrics about flowers.

The thing to remember about *Transformer* is that Reed is not coming out of the closet. The album takes it for granted that we know he's a queer. Instead, he's eager to unsettle our image of what that means. "You must think I'm some kinda gay blade," sneers Lou, seeming to consider the flamboyant homosexual as one of the lowest forms of human life. Or maybe he just hates being typified, characterized. If for one second you thought Lou Reed was a categorizable stereotype, he has no sympathy for you. "You want me to hit you with a stick," he says to anyone who expects the sadomasochistic sexual references he's become known for singing about and rumored to engage in. "But all I've got's a guitar pick." He insists: I'm just a musician, not the freakish deviant you came to see. My violence is musical, cultural, the opposite of whatever you wanted.

Nonetheless, the lyrics turn explicitly violent as the song goes on. The contempt in this song is disturbing in its force, far beyond your average "get offa my cloud" sentiment. "I step on your hands and I mangle your feet," Lou sings twice. His lover/enemy, who hit him with a flower, is now crawling on the ground, and Reed mercilessly breaks his fingers. I don't even want to think about what kind of violence it takes to mangle someone's feet. What's provoking such intense rage at the outset of this record?

The antisocial sentiment in this song clusters around sexuality. "When I watch you come, baby I just want to run."

He is disgusted, even panicked, by someone else's sexual pleasure. Sexuality has become an arena of fear and shame, pushing him to savage brutality. He sarcastically mocks the tepid feminine attacker who wields a flower, and at the same time codedly confesses that it is the soft petals of feminine sexuality that truly make him feel threatened.

Here, making his glam rock debut, Lou Reed has to somehow address the problems of gender and sexuality which have caused him so much turmoil. His only defense is to deny the terms of the conversation, saying "fuck you" to anyone who thinks they have him figured out—particularly straight people who think they understand what it means to be gay.

This is an understandable sentiment at a cultural moment when Lou's homosexuality, rather than a socially unacceptable open secret, is suddenly his selling point. A few times in this period, Lou Reed expressed varying levels of contempt for all the straight or "confused" male glam rock fans who experimented with homosexuality or gender-bending behavior. "You can't fake being gay," he said in a 1973 interview with Lester Bangs, at the height of his association with homosexuality as a hip pose.

The makeup thing is just a style thing now, like platform shoes. If people have homosexuality in them, it won't necessarily involve makeup in the first place. You can't fake being gay, because being gay means you're going to have to suck cock, or get fucked. I think there's a very basic thing in a guy if he's straight where he's just going to say no: "I'll act gay, I'll do this and I'll do that, but I can't do *that*."

You can feel him flirting with how much contempt to express. Later in the interview he gets more explicitly disdainful. Bangs writes:

> When I asked him about his plans for his next album, he said: "I may come out with a hardhat album. Come out with an anti-gay song, saying 'Get back in your closets, you fuckin' queers!' That'll really do it!"
>
> But let's just suppose that Lou Reed is gay. If he is, can you imagine what kind of homosexual would say something like that? Maybe that's what makes him such a master of the pop song—he's got such a great sense of *shame*.

Bangs is right; this is part of what makes him so good. His anger is directed inward as much as outward, and the resultant friction creates the sparks that power these songs. It's clear by the midpoint of "Vicious" that it's the speaker himself that is the vicious one, stepping on hands and mangling feet. He's talking to himself, and this hatred, like a lot of hatred this intense, is self-hatred—one of the secret themes of this album.

But despite all that, this song might still be partly about Andy Warhol, perhaps the effeminate homosexual dearest to Lou. The song was, after all, an assignment Andy gave him.[1] Lou told *Rolling Stone* in 1989: "Andy said, 'Why don't you write a song called "Vicious"?' I said, 'Well, Andy, what kind of vicious?' 'Oh, you know, like I hit you with a flower.'"

---

[1] In the early seventies Andy produced a number of theater plays, and he asked Lou to write some songs for a musical he was planning to produce in collaboration with fashion designer Yves Saint Laurent. More on that later.

And I wrote it down, literally. Because I kept a notebook in those days. I used it for poetry and things people said."[2] In Reed's hands, Warhol's casually suggested idea becomes an outlet for all the unresolved pain of their stormy love-hate friendship and collaboration. Its status as inspired by Andy and possibly directed at Andy offers no resolution, but only intensifies the two artists' ambiguous relationship.

"Vicious" fades out and gives way to an oblique ode to Warhol, the bewildering "Andy's Chest," confirming the semi-covert influence of Lou's ex-mentor on the album. Here *Transformer* doubles down on its primary aim: to frustrate, to tease, to dare you to look for meaning, figuring you won't but hoping you will.

[2]Bockris, *Transformer*, 200.

"Andy's Chest"
Lou and Warhol

First of all, the relevant historical information:

Andy Warhol was shot in the chest on June 3, 1968 by his friend/associate Valerie Solanas, at the Factory. She was a radical feminist writer, an early proponent of lesbian separatism, and wrote the infamous SCUM Manifesto, which is as vitriolic and extreme a statement against the entirety of the male gender as could be imagined. (SCUM stands for Society for Cutting Up Men.) Solanas had also appeared in the Warhol-directed film *I, A Man*. After asking him to return a theater script she had given him to read and being indifferently told it had been misplaced, Solanas shot at Warhol three times, hitting him once. He was in intensive care for weeks, and barely survived; she was jailed for three years. After this, Warhol became more cautious and intensified security measures at the Factory to protect himself. The general consensus among his friends is that the scene was never the same after the shooting.

Reed wrote this song not long afterward as *some* sort of response to the event. It's definitely affectionate, which may have been emotionally important at the time. Warhol and Reed had had something of a falling out in 1967, resulting in Warhol being dismissed as the Velvet Underground's manager. This song might have functioned as a peacemaking gesture from Lou to Andy. The Velvet Underground recorded a version of the song in the summer of 1969 as part of an album that MGM, their record label, ended up refusing to release—under new management that year, MGM purged its roster of acts that had failed to significantly profit the label, so the Velvets and their just-recorded album were lost in the shuffle. The Velvets' version of "Andy's Chest," played at a faster clip than the *Transformer* version and sounding a little manically unfocused (notice the charmingly bizarre choice of a Chet Atkins-style guitar solo), was eventually released in 1985 as part of the compilation album *VU*, which included tracks from the lost MGM album as well as other rarities.

It used to frustrate me that this particular song was the unreleased VU track Reed and Bowie chose to resurrect. For years it was my least favorite song on both *Transformer* and *VU*. To the casual ear, the lyrics sound about as sophisticated as a schoolyard nonsense chant. "Now when people say her feet smell, they mean her nose." Is this really supposed to be one of the greatest songwriters of the century?

The closer I listen, the more I've started to come around to it. For one thing, it's just a sweet, offbeat, bizarre little love song to a friend, if that's all you want from it. That's enough to make it a good song, and it allows you to leave it at that, no questions asked.

But for the person who takes these things too seriously—you reading this, me writing it, and anyone who wants to place Lou Reed into some pantheon of Great Artists Worthy Of Study—it teasingly intimates shades of sophistication, hidden tunnels that may or may not be of any great depth. As in the children's song "Ring Around the Rosy"—popularly rumored to reference the Great Plague of London—or the sanitized Disney film versions of the Grimms' fairy tales, the childish content masks a more complex and dark history. What sounds like a twee collection of lazy rhymes also turns out to be one artist talking about a contemporary's wounded body, and connecting it with images of classical art: Roman noblemen, Christian soldiers, knights in flaming silver robes. Not only that, but it's a friend and perhaps frustrated lover pretending to write a song about an uncomplicated affection, and seeming to fool even himself. Like the album as a whole, the track is somehow both dumbly unsubtle and so nuanced that its full meaning ducks out of our view.

This is kind of a magic trick. Lou Reed can write a sloppy, near-moronic song and manage to have it also be a culturally significant artwork. The same dynamic that vexes the museum-goer who scowls at a minimalist abstract painting, saying, "my four-year-old could do that," may also bother someone listening to rock music in the early seventies as it grows in critical acclaim and consideration. Both Andy Warhol and Lou Reed flaunt the simplicity and ease of what they do: it's easy to reprint a photo of Elvis Presley or to make up silly "nose-toes" rhymes. But when it's branded with the name Andy Warhol or Lou Reed, it's Art. It's the name, not the craft, and these artists are not virtuosos, they're celebrities.

This song is branded with both of their names, and thus associates the culture of "high art" with the low-art world of rock 'n' roll. Of course, one of Warhol's roles in the history of art was as a great merger of the high and low. Reed was a major part of the same process, but from the other direction: the forced conversion, over the course of the sixties, of pop songwriting into high art. By the time this record comes around, categories like "low" and "high" are getting less and less meaningful when it comes to art, which may be why he gets away with lyrics this dumb, or "dumb." Once you can put a picture of a Campbell's soup can in a museum, all bets are off.

The trickier question here is: What's with the title? How does this collection of absurdist imagery relate to Andy Warhol being shot?

One possibility is that the title of the song is, along with the lyrics, a free-associative non sequitur that was chosen out of laziness or playful Dada insouciance. In the same mode as, say, Bob Dylan's "Rainy Day Women Nos. 12 & 35," the song was named after a phrase that was kicking around in the songwriter's head and had just enough personal resonance to seem satisfying as a title. One could make a strong case for this. Calling it "Andy's Chest" does do a few useful things to the song. For one, it connects it with Andy Warhol, reminding us of Lou Reed's seal of approval from the art world along with his celebrity social life. On a less insider level, it suggests that the song is about a man's body, giving it the intrigue of being a same-sex love song—perfect for *Transformer* and glam rock. So the title may not make total sense, but it kind of associatively puts you in the early-seventies Lou Reed world of art, fame, and homosexuality.

I reject this interpretation, the one that would chalk the title up to sloppy quasi-randomness. I don't think there are any accidents here. In fact, I think art in general tends to be mostly devoid of pure accident. I've been writing songs long enough to know that when you think you've written a song that's basically about nothing, a string of phrases that seemed evocative or cool to you in the moment of composition but are basically meaningless, you've probably obliquely uncovered something that's taking up a large section of your subconscious. In freely writing nonsense, as Lou may seem to be doing here, you plow up the dirt in your head and find what's hiding underneath. As he put it in a 2001 TV documentary on *Transformer*, "I find out what the songs are about when I do them out loud in front of an audience. . . . But I could be wrong. Just because I wrote it doesn't mean I know what it's about."[1]

What did Andy's chest look like? It was a huge fucking scar. The doctors had to cut his chest open and massage his failing heart to revive him. Lou Reed knows about scars. Andy's physical scar resonates with Lou's emotional scars, and Andy's brush with death on the operating table with Lou's convulsive seizures while strapped to the electroshock therapy table. Lou consistently expressed enormous affection and sympathy for Andy throughout his adult life, and this song is that kind of love song: I know you've been hurt, friend; so have I. Don't let 'em get to you. You're the greatest.

Lou saw Andy get a lot of backlash from the public, and absorbed some of it himself. The Velvet Underground were often dismissed as one of Andy Warhol's willfully obtuse pop

---

[1]*Classic Albums: Transformer*. Directed by Bob Smeaton. United Kingdom: Isis Productions, 2001. Full disclosure: he was talking about "Satellite of Love," but his point stands as generalizable to any of his songs.

art experiments. Once, in their favorite bar, Max's Kansas City, an enraged drunk threw a table at Andy, which missed him and hit Lou, knocking him down and bruising him badly.[2] Hanging out with Andy made Lou Reed famous, bringing fame's attendant adoration and hatred along with it.

Interviewed by John Wilcock for a book about Warhol published in 1971,[3] Lou said:

> Andy's gone through the most incredible suffering. They let her [Solanas] off with three years. You get more for stealing a car. It's just unbelievable. But the point is the hatred directed at him by society was really reflected. . . . Most very big people seem to have enemies, and seem to be getting shot, which is something a lot of people should keep in mind. There is a lot to be said for not being in the limelight.

Spoken in the early seventies, as Lou very haltingly circles his potential for rock stardom, trying to decide when and whether to strike, this sheds some light on his view of fame. Fame was a laugh to Warhol, an arty experiment, until it nearly got him killed. One can imagine Reed's ambivalence, and the temptation to go back home and work a quiet, normal job. "All the venom snipers after you," he sings to his poor famous friend. "All the cheap bloodsuckers are flying after you." Can you blame him if at times he wants no part of it?

* * *

[2]Bockris, *Transformer,* 141–42.
[3]Ibid., 159.

Nevertheless, this track is the sound of him taking his part in it, trying for a hit record and superstardom. An old abandoned Velvet Underground song mutates into a Bowie/Ronson production, rendering Lou Reed scarcely recognizable to his old friends. "When Lou went solo, he got bad and was copying people," said Andy himself.[4] This jab, in the context of the two artists' perpetually contentious friendship/rivalry, must have stung in its truthful Warholian ultra-simplicity. Lou's mentor was right. Having erased his old band and his old self, Lou Reed As Rock Star was an empty frame waiting to be filled in by whatever aesthetic made the strongest claim on it. That turned out to be '72 Bowie, that is, basically Ziggy Stardust & the Spiders From Mars. Through this filter, Reed turned into the powdered, contrast-dialed-up Mick Rock cover photograph, often seeming more like an icon than a fully fleshed-out human artist.

This is something he now shared with David Bowie: the sense of artifice, the sense of fame for fame's sake, an increased distance from the audience. An image, behind which there was either nothing at all or something that didn't matter because it wasn't part of the performance. This element does not encapsulate either artist, but in their 1972 incarnations it was the dominant story they were telling about themselves. These were not human beings, they were stars. Perhaps what the cover of *Transformer* most evokes, with Lou's dead eyes and frightening presentation, is a Frankenstein's monster, as does this particular stage of his career. Having assembled a body from the lifeless tissue of the departed Velvet

[4]Ibid., 211.

Underground, Bowie the mad doctor will harness the power of his own fame to bring his dark dreams to fruition. A career that was dead will now live.

"Andy's Chest" and "Satellite of Love" are Bowie and Ronson's most transparent efforts to reanimate their own bastardized version of Lou Reed. These are particularly obvious fix-up jobs because we have documents of what these songs looked like in the full flush of their natural lives: the Velvet Underground recorded both of them. The Velvets' version of "Andy's Chest" has a charmingly casual feel: a playful bass guitar jumps from low to high notes while the drums barrel along like the "George of the Jungle" cartoon's theme song, and a cheery guitar solo intervenes.

In the *Transformer* version—as happened to a lot of music as the sixties became the seventies and pop bands gave way to heavy rock music—the tempo has slowed, the bass is bassier, the toms are more present in the mix. It's all simultaneously a bit more self-assured and a bit more plodding. It's cooler, in a way, but it's also become oddly top-heavy, the band a lumbering giant who may be about to slowly fall flat on its face. I don't fault the drop in tempo—it crucially allows Lou to actually sing phrases like "a dentured ocelot on a leash" rather than rush through them like an auctioneer—but the track has sacrificed its predecessor's likeable sense of tossed-off play. The more self-serious Bowie production ironically contrasts with the silly lyrics, making one wonder if indeed Lou is trying to say something serious here. The longish, quiet intro gives way to a dramatic drum fill, announcing, "This is Important. This is an Event." Is this, we may legitimately wonder, supposed to be some kind of Ziggy Stardustian

Major Statement? Or was the whole Ziggy thing an absurdist prank the whole time?

But this song, regardless of which band is behind Lou, is fundamentally a confusion of high and low, serious art and playful joke, which is something that could be said of Andy Warhol's whole career, as well as Reed's and Bowie's, at least up to that point. Of course it's absurd to be famous for printing a photograph of a can of soup, just as ridiculous as getting hundreds of thousands of people to listen to you sing "you have a hairy-minded pink bare bear." Bowie and Ronson know this and are having fun with it; you can hear the sarcasm in their "ba ba ba ba baaaaaa" backup vocals. You can picture them dressed in sequined leotards, lined up with the Rockettes doing the can-can at Radio City Music Hall. It's all a little ridiculous on this song. But as with a lot of Bowie music, and po-mo art in general, the ridiculous blends seamlessly with the sense that you are watching a Major Artist make a Major Statement.

"The whole glam thing was kind of great for me, when I met Bowie and he was into that, and so I got into that," Lou told an interviewer in the late eighties.

But all it was, was it was something I had already seen with Warhol. But I hadn't done that. So the seventies was like, a chance for me to get in on it, and since no one knew me from Adam particularly, I could say I was anything, be any way. . . . I learned that from Andy. You could be anything.[5]

---

[5] *Lou Reed Remembered*, 32:20. Directed by Chris Rodley. United Kingdom: BBC 4, 2013.

At the start of a reinvention of his music career, Lou kept in mind that Andy Warhol had taught him the fundamental possibility of self-invention. Andy inspired him and helped him develop a self that worked for him: one that was allowed to be weird, allowed to be gay, allowed to be an artist. Keep in mind that Lou was twenty-three years old when they met, only recently out of college. Warhol was a great permissive force in his life, as well as the major influence that legitimized the Velvet Underground and made them a viable, respected entity.

But this song is not "If you can dream it, you can become it." It's a concise little phantasmagoria of gruesome mutilations and magical transformations that seem to happen by accident. The same might be said of the whole album. The sense of free association, of easily sliding from punk rock to cabaret to accessible pop music, is part of the plan. Writing a rambling, nonsensical lyric is one way of telling your audience that they have and are failing to fully understand you. It destabilizes their sense of where the meaning in your work lies, and that destabilization opens the possibility of transformation.

He needs that possibility to stay open. In this career reinvention, his identity has not been simply changed, it *is* change. He becomes something new, but it ultimately doesn't stick; it ends up being as awkward as his hands becoming his feet. If he transforms into a Bowie-ish glam rock star now, he will hurriedly transform into something entirely different on the next album, and again on the next one, and the next one after that.

"If I could be anything," Lou begins. A pregnant opening line for a moment in his career when he's in bad need of a new beginning. But he doesn't say pop star, he doesn't say beauty queen, he says, "I would be a bat." As the song proceeds, Reed quickly builds in lyrics a fantasy counter-world where anything can turn into anything else. It's both whimsical and a little frightening, a nursery rhyme with a touch of the gothic: "You know what happens after dark / when rattlesnakes lose their skins and their hearts." Superimposed over all of it is the massive scar across Andy's chest—the mutilations of fame. What will happen to me, our long-underrated hero wonders, when I finally stand in this elusive spotlight for which I've lusted so bitterly?

He doesn't know. What he does know is that he's come a long way from suburbia, and whatever he changes into next, he owes it all to Andy. "Bats that with a kiss turn prince, for you." This horror story just might become a fairy tale, and maybe "Vicious" was a kind of love song after all.

If this liminal ambiguity of mood frustrates you, I'm afraid the next song won't provide much relief.

"Perfect Day"
Lou and Bettye

Lou Reed met twenty-year-old Bettye Kronstadt, supposedly at a department store, in the late sixties, though their romance didn't begin until late summer 1970. He had quit the Velvet Underground and, in a complex mood of shame and hopefulness, returned to live in his parents' house and at last work for his father's accounting firm, a career move his parents had been pleading him to make for years. In crisis, he was looking for a savior, someone to love him who had no connection to the world of downtown dirt and drug abuse he'd left behind. She emerged, reportedly,[1] from a rack

---

[1] I read this detail in multiple Lou Reed biographies, only to find another one with an irreconcilable story about the couple meeting while visiting a mutual friend in the hospital. I am starting to notice how rampant the problem of unattributed quotes, un-cited sources, unverifiable information, etc. is in writing about music. Lou Reed in particular encourages ambiguities and promotes falsehoods about himself, and fans (and even friends) of his tend to have a habit of seeing him how they want to see him, twisting facts to fit their powerful image of him. I'm making an effort at accuracy, but we are dealing with an avowed shape-shifter. This book is necessarily about Lou Reed's mythology as much as his reality, and the two may blur together from time to time.

of dresses at Bloomingdale's, wearing pearls and makeup, a nice, drug-free Jewish girl, also from Long Island, whom his parents would approve of.

To be fair, Lou was drawn to Bettye just as much for her intellect, passion for the arts, and bohemian leanings. A student at Columbia, taking creative writing classes and acting classes, she was definitely suitably arty for his taste. She was an activist with on-campus groups and had been involved in protests that led to clashes with local police. She had even auditioned to be a dancer for Andy Warhol's Exploding Plastic Inevitable show, where she might have ended up meeting Lou years earlier had she got the gig. Like Lou, she was a kid from the suburbs who had come to blossom in the city, rebelling against the older generation while still remaining attached to her parents. In her acting classes, she went by the name Krista. She, too, was trying to remake herself, along with the rest of America's liberal youth at the end of the sixties, and unsure how far to take it. The romance began with Lou commuting by train from Freeport, Long Island into the city, or her out to him. They ping-ponged back and forth, physically and psychically, between the infinite possible lives New York City represented and the comfort of their childhood homes where a stable identity had been planned for them.

Despite her measure of bohemian cred, she still came off as a very conservative choice of partner for the famously debaucherous Lou Reed, largely because of two facts: one, she was a woman, and two, she didn't do drugs. Reed was trying to shed his identity as a gay drug addict musician and become a heterosexual, sober 9-to-5-er. Bettye fit the bill perfectly, and he idealized her to destructive effect. "Some part of Lou really does like stability and the old cozy kitchen and homey living rooms," commented Sterling Morrison.[2] Or as Lou put it: "Bettye is not hip at all, and I want to keep her that way. . . . I believe in pretty princesses."[3]

This woman would become his wife early in 1973. Over the following year or so, the relationship deteriorated into domestic violence and eventual divorce. Reed repeatedly abused Kronstadt physically and emotionally. Bettye tells how "he gave me a black eye the second time he hit me. . . . Everybody knew he was abusive."[4] And the couple's shared attempt to end Reed's alcohol and amphetamine abuse failed entirely: Reed was addicted to both drugs for the ensuing ten years. But to the not-yet-married Lou and Bettye, in their twenties, it must have seemed quite plausible that Lou was leaving behind his tumultuous underworld existence and settling down for a Quiet, Normal Life.

So this is the period when they have their Perfect Day. They meet in Central Park on a summer night, drink sangria, and go to a movie. They are newly in love and life is beautiful, and why can't they have their simple, idyllic afternoon? Never mind the years of drug use, never mind the sixties burning out in a violent tailspin, never mind the police harassment and the personal turmoil and the electroshock therapy. It's just a perfect day. Problems all left alone.

[2]Bockris, *Transformer*, 183.
[3]Ibid.
[4]Reed, *Waiting For The Man*, 61.

Reed reaches a moment of genius with this song that rivals anything in his career.[5] But it's not the bombastic sonic adventurousness of "Heroin" or the masterful verbal outpour of late-career coups like "Dirty Blvd." It's a song with few words and an elegant, traditional arrangement musically recalling the kind of torch song that Billie Holiday might have sung decades earlier. The chord sequence, starting in the key of A-minor, evokes an overhanging mood of sadness. On the phrase "perfect day," the verse lifts via a D chord and finds the relative major key of C for a fleetingly pleasant moment (always landing on an lyric image suggesting escape: "in the park," "in the zoo," "forget myself," etc.) before it descends back into the more familiar sadness of the original key.

The lyrics, too, optimistically describe a beautiful, simple scene, but very gradually let in more and more complex darkness. "Then later, when it gets dark," Reed sings in the first verse, suggesting doom to come. The "animals in the zoo" evoke imprisonment and the whole lyrical milieu gently but

---

[5]It pains me to call this man a genius just as I acknowledge his spouse abuse. He habitually attacked a woman who loved him and, being eight years younger than him and much less established as an artist, probably looked up to him. It makes me ethically uncomfortable to write this book, and it probably should cause you some discomfort to read it, and even to call yourself a Lou Reed fan. I am willing to praise a man who has done terrible things. I refuse to deny the power of art because of the moral violations committed by its creator. However, I respect those who turn away from art made by sometimes-reprehensible people. It's a personal choice that is difficult for me, but in the end I am able to embrace the art even as I condemn the artist, though not without also confronting some real ethical ambiguity.

overpoweringly tells us that the perfection has been destroyed by intervening tragedy. "Problems all left alone" ups the tension in the second verse—the problems aren't gone, they're just left elsewhere for later. Thus we are emotionally primed for the punch line: "I thought I was someone else / Someone good."

The chorus is the grand major-key attempt at happiness, and, matching the lyrics perfectly, it keeps us hanging on: the song suddenly sounds like the triumph of light over darkness, good over evil. Maybe we're hearing a full-hearted, exultant love song after all, and not a dirge. But then the singer's voice turns mournful again, and we are once more trapped in the verses' dark shadows.

This song is one of Lou Reed's greatest moments of subtlety and nuance, when he lives up to the linguistic pithiness of Raymond Chandler which he has often praised in interviews. It's a song that convinces you it's talking about one thing and simultaneously suggests that it's talking about something else entirely, like a hostage struggling to speak calmly over the phone with a gun pointed at their head. Randy Newman has often written in a similarly subtle mode—present the bare facts with just enough spin to show the twisted sublimated situation—but always nodding toward a dark joke rather than an unbearable inner crisis. "Perfect Day" has few peers.

The only precedent I can really think of for a song this laconically ambiguous, this secretly wounded, is another Lou Reed song, the Velvet Underground song "Sunday Morning." Like "Perfect Day," it directs the listener in two opposite lines of thought at once. In both cases, you can't actually tell exactly what kind of song you're listening to. What is the content or cause of the "restless feeling," "a feeling I don't want to know," described in the lyrics of "Sunday Morning?" The singer doesn't say. The music, too, goes both ways: comforting and ominous, gentle and threatening. The childlike celeste of the earlier song is analogous to the sentimental string section of the later one, both evoking a tender optimism that cannot last in such close proximity to the enveloping darkness. Ironically for someone so often described as being a guy who can write but can't sing, good with words but simplistic or clumsy with music, in both these songs Reed's delivery is everything. There aren't, in fact, many words at all. The effect depends on the musical setting and the expertly expressive vocal. Both move from a quiet fragility to a desperate, faltering attempt at healthful exultation, then defeatedly back to fragility.

What's so painful in this succinct little tune has a lot to do with who Lou Reed is in the early seventies, who he would like to be and who he can never be. What would a perfect day look like? What would life be like if not for the demons he never seems to finish exorcising? Why, he might fall in love. He and his girl might go, simply, to the park, to a movie. He might be able to attain all the romantic clichés marketed to him when he was growing up in his favorite jazz standards and sangria-sweet doo-wop ballads. He might be someone else, someone good. In other words, he might be straight.

He sees the whole heterosexual dream-cliché rise and fall in front of his eyes in a single afternoon. He lives it for a few hours and knows it cannot last. It's not that he doesn't want the dream. It's that he's not the person for whom it was designed, and he never will be. He's too gay and too fucked-up and too angry for this perfect day to be anything but a momentary aberration in his life.

Through the queer lens, the whole opaque song starts to make more sense and take on greater resonance. Out of context of who the singer is, that refrain, "you just keep me hanging on," feels emotionally apt but logically bewildering. I guess he's talking about unrequited love, I thought when I first heard the song, unaware of the bisexual turmoil that birthed this record. I guess they're just friends but he wants it to be more. But even on first listen, I could feel that this line was somehow more troubled than that. The longing in the climactic descending chords is permanent, existential. The singer can never have this happiness, but the object of his love continually holds it in front of his face, insisting that it's possible. Don't give up, Lou. We can have the ideal straight life we were brought up to ache for. We can be Normal.

No we can't, the song concludes, and you're going to pay for torturing me like this. For drawing me into this impossible love that cannot work out, for planting and re-planting this poisonous seed in my brain. You're going to reap just what you sow. At this vengeful utterance, the musically conflicted, continually shifting chord progression reaches a soothing resolution in the key of A-major, a key which the chorus had attempted but never sustained. There is no comfort, the whole structure of the song asserts, in these fleeting moments of happiness. The narrator reaches satisfaction only at the promise of emotional retribution.

* * *

Two songs in, we thought we knew what kind of record we were listening to: some sort of offbeat version of tough-guy rock music; an unusual songwriter with a hell of a band behind him.

You'd expect a ballad to show up at some point, but "Perfect Day" is surprising in its delicate tenderness and its incongruous drama. Is this really the guy from "Vicious," now drinking sangria in the park and going to the zoo? Is this his band? It sounds more like Judy Garland's. What happened to the guitar?

Here we start to see what a powerhouse Mick Ronson is. What happened to the guitar is that the guy playing it can also come up with and play a brilliant piano part. He did the string arrangement, too. Ronson is so good, I assert, that Reed's career would have looked a lot different had they never met. This is Reed's first true musical success that goes beyond what a garage band might do. Ronson and Bowie, on this album, teach Lou to have faith in production, that is, in making songs with accoutrements beyond pure rock 'n' roll. *Berlin*, the epic follow-up to *Transformer*, wouldn't have happened if these young Brits hadn't showed him that orchestral arrangements could suit his songs perfectly, bringing out their sophistication and drama. Without Ronson in particular, it might have been pure three-chord garage rock for the rest of Lou's life. With Ronson, Lou learns to sound as ambitious as he is really is.

I'd go so far as to say that *Berlin* is "Perfect Day" stretched to the length of a full album. This track predicts that whole fascinating record: the orchestration, the bombast, the romance on the verge of collapse, the suppressed rage, and the looming tragedy. This song functions in the same way as, or even better than, the song "Berlin," both a musical and a conceptual prelude to the emotional devastation that ensues when someone like the young Lou Reed gets married. It could have been the first track on *Berlin*. Just sayin'.

"Hangin' 'Round"
Lou and Coolness

There are so many ways to say "fuck you." This is one of Lou Reed's great messages to the world. You can shoot heroin and withdraw from society. You can take speed and play guitar really loud. You can unabashedly break sexual taboos. You can respond to a public who wants you to be one thing by being the exact opposite. You can get belligerent, nasty, and violent. You can fail despite everyone who expects you to succeed, or you can succeed despite everyone who expects you to fail.

Or you can say "get the fuck away from me," as does "Hangin' 'Round." Half-heartedly pretending to be a literary character-based song populated by intriguing denizens of the underworld like "Sister Ray" or "Wild Side," it is in fact a list of (not very well-drawn) characters whom Lou Reed is cooler than, followed by the recurrent chorus expressing annoyance at their presence. It lacks the novelistic acuity of a true Lou Reed classic, and ends up sounding like filler, propping up the album's intention of passing as a rock 'n' roll record (an identity destabilized by a surprising number of showtune-esque piano- and tuba-dependent tracks: "Perfect

Day," "Make Up," "New York Telephone Conversation," "Goodnight Ladies." More on that later.)

Another interesting failing of this song is that it shows none of the compassion for which Reed's songwriting is often praised—a compassion which, in my opinion, is in fact rather rare in his catalog, at least in the first twenty years of his career.[1] I suspect that his refusal to condemn the characters he writes about has often been mistaken for empathy with them. Most people talking or writing about drag queens or drug addicts in the sixties and seventies had, subtly or not, some negative judgment of those people's character to offer. Lou Reed did not, and for that I respect him. He did, however, write lines like "When someone turns that blue, well it's a universal truth / And then you know that bitch will never fuck again" ("Street Hassle," 1977). Not a very empathetic thing to say when a woman overdoses at your apartment. Sure, he's writing in the voice of a character (we hope), but clearly he's at least as interested in cold-hearted misanthropy as he is in compassion.[2]

---

[1] Lester Bangs lovingly called him, in 1979, "a person with deep compassion for a great many other people about whom almost nobody else gives a shit." Lester Bangs, "Lou Reed: The Bells," *Rolling Stone*, June 14, 1979.

[2] The real thing I think people are trying to articulate when they praise Reed's compassion is the fact that in his best work (of which "Hangin' 'Round" is not an example), he tends to *take people seriously* when he writes about them. He's not sentimental and he's not sanctimonious; he's plainly honest about the strange or dark places people can end up. His tone of inhuman apathy is usually a strategic literary device which gets the listener's attention and sets her up to notice what's interesting or emotional about the story he's telling. He's not always compassionate toward his underworld characters,

Some of the roots of this misanthropy, which would grow more and more extreme over the course of the sixties, can be found on Velvet Underground records, but *Transformer* is where it becomes one of his signature moves. "Hangin' 'Round" (along with "New York Telephone Conversation") is a sort of light, "fun" version of his smoldering sociopathy, one you can still laugh at, whereas "Vicious" is a little more worrying of a step toward total psychopathy. Cathy with the painted toes who won't let anyone smoke while she's in the room *does* sound irritating. But when you find out that the real Lou Reed was habitually beating the shit out of his fiancée, it stops being such a laugh.

Regardless of the disturbing personal scoop on the singer, this is the kind of aggressive uptempo music most

but he *sees* them, which is notable and powerful in the context of a society that prefers to ignore them.

Here he is in a 1989 interview, showing his cards as a songwriter with the striking self-awareness typical of his later career:

> I think sometimes things carry more of an emotional wallop if when you tell it you're a bit detached. It'll catch people a bit off guard. They're not looking for that. And I also think that it makes things sound true. Because you're not trying to impress them, you're not trying to make them cry, you're not trying to make them sad, you're not trying to make them scared. You're telling them a story in a straightforward way. (*Lou Reed Remembered*, 22:30. Directed by Chris Rodley. United Kingdom: BBC 4, 2013.)

"Street Hassle," by the way, *is* among his best work, and the heartless line I quoted from it is soon followed by what may be his moment of greatest compassion for people who have lost their way after being abused by society. So, fine, maybe the old bastard wasn't all bad, after all.

of us signed up for when we bought the record. After the ambiguous light/dark mood of "Perfect Day" with its out-of-character orchestral approach, we return with relief to the main attraction: good old-fashioned fuck-you rock 'n' roll.

But then, Velvet Underground fans may notice a tameness to *Transformer*'s brand of uptempo rock. This simple tough-guy music reminds you of "Waiting for the Man" or "Run Run Run," but it's in fact considerably more polished and rhythmically easygoing, its raw impact neutralized. When the classic glam rock bands played their more aggressive songs, the rhythm section would heavily "swing" the beat, emphasizing the backbeat: "one-and-TWO-and-three-and-FOUR-and." You can hear this on T. Rex's "Get it On," David Bowie's "Suffragette City," Gary Glitter's "Rock and Roll (Parts 1 & 2)." This is the rhythmic mode of "Hangin' 'Round," and the result is a song that makes you want to dance, moving your body in a way that reflects the snare drum's pauses and accents. Whereas the Velvet Underground would swing considerably less on the fast songs, with bass and drums relentlessly hitting on every beat of every measure: "ONE-TWO-THREE-FOUR-ONE-TWO-THREE-FOUR." When that kind of rhythm's playing, as in "Waiting For the Man," you don't want to roll your shoulders and move your hips, you want to tense up and bang your head on every beat. It's the tense, hyper-speed pace of New York, the city that never sleeps, especially if you're on amphetamines.

The early Velvet Underground would have done "Hangin' 'Round" more justice: it ought to be amateurish and antisocial, as is the songwriting. Instead, crunchy guitars notwithstanding, it's a lot more cheerful and professional, the lead guitar inflecting its careful phrases upward and the bass player politely grooving rather than pounding along unstoppably. The intention here is transparently to recapture some of that VU sonic mojo and repackage it for a larger audience. The attempt is both successful and not: it's loud, it's fun, but a basic New York purity of rage has disappeared.

Plus, you can't miss the tepid quality of this particular kiss-off. "I'm not so glad you found me." If he's trying to do another "Vicious," he's definitely dialed down the rage; no longer hoping for your untimely death, he's simply "not so glad" to see you. Which isn't surprising, is in fact characteristic: understatement has always been as much a part of his approach to songwriting and performing as has extreme transgression. When the two are in ironic tension with each other, the effect is to make him seem unflappably cool and unhampered by pretense.

And that leads us to the real subject of this song: how much cooler than you Lou Reed is. Because *Transformer* inaugurates the stage of Lou's career when he becomes literally too cool to function. He's so beyond giving a shit that some nights he can't even stand up onstage. That is, of course, due to alcohol and speed abuse, but his use of those substances is inseparable from his self-conception as a rock star who lives by his own rules. He will be addicted to both drugs until the early eighties, when he makes a more earnest attempt at a stable marriage and starts presenting himself as a mellowed, thoughtful elder statesman. Which is to say, once he releases his grip on identifying as a particular kind of Cool. For now, he's so cool, so bored, so wasted that he sounds barely committed to the lazy lyrics he's written.

Still, this song contains one of the lines that could be the epigraph that sums up the whole album, perhaps printed in scare quotes on the back of the sleeve: "You're still doing things that I gave up years ago."

I'm struck by how simultaneously simple and ambiguous this refrain is. On first listen, the line doesn't make much impact; its dismissive boredom is a bland, kind of obvious posture for a rock star to assume. But once he says it a couple times you start to wonder exactly what he means. Is he bragging that he's gone further out into depravity, is more freely adventurous with sex and drugs and rock 'n' roll, than the person he's addressing? Or, more likely, has he tried everything and at this point is *so over it*? Having written "Heroin" in the mid-sixties, is Lou, in the early seventies, flirting with sobriety, monogamy, heterosexuality?

Well, yes, if his biography is any indication. He did just get married—to a woman—who doesn't do drugs. The sixties are over, and Lou has transgressed every boundary of straight society. Having done that, the last frontier is normality. Or if not the last frontier, the last symbol of a lost childhood, for which he now desperately grasps, knowing it's unattainable. Either way, he's finally seeming to settle down in his private life, which makes this a profoundly weird time for him to unveil himself to the pop scene as the queen of the fringe urban underworld.

So you get a song like "Hangin' 'Round," where he faces the deep irony of being marketed as the ultimate bohemian just as he's outgrown it all. In the chorus, he could easily be talking to David Bowie, and all the music fans who are shocked and delighted by the glam rockers' performative breaking of sexual and gender taboos. Lou may not be so glad they found him, after all. He didn't ask to be discovered by these rich kids who fetishize his drug addiction and bisexuality.

Asked by British music magazine *Melody Maker* about the Velvet Underground's shocking lyrical themes, Lou said in 1972, "What I was writing about was just what was going on around me. I didn't realise it was a whole new world for everybody else. Everybody else is now in the point I was in 1967. Makes me wonder where they'll be in five years' time. Come to that, makes me wonder where I'm at now."[3] Even through the arrogance, this sounds to me like an honest statement. He really doesn't know. Is he settling into a stable adulthood, or is he about to relapse into the debauchery he so disdains in this song?

As it turned out, he relapsed. The marriage didn't last and he never stayed sober for long. But what interests me is how his need to seem cooler than everyone else pushes him toward a kind of conservatism. We remember him on the third Velvets record singing softly, "Jesus, help me find my proper place." Not at all the cool thing to do in 1969, but that's just it: no one expected it. On "Hangin' 'Round," he quotes "Hark! the Herald Angels Sing" with a wink; later, on the second side of the record, he'll more solemnly intone, "Heavenly Father, I know I have sinned." This is how committed Reed is to defying your expectations. Just when you think you know him, he'll turn Christian.

---

[3] Reed, *Waiting For The Man*, 64.

Ultimately, being Cool is just a way for Lou to elude a firm identity. Once it's what he's known for, he'll ditch that too. He doesn't hang around, he moves on before you've even had a chance to wrap your head around what he's doing. The Velvet Underground broke up before you ever heard of them. He's on speed, baby, and you'll never catch up with him.

"Walk on the Wild Side"
Lou and the Underworld

Cast of Characters (in order of appearance)

Holly Woodlawn: Born in Juana Diaz, Puerto Rico, and raised mostly in Miami, Florida, Holly bused and hitchhiked to New York City in 1963 at the age of fifteen. She had been designated male at birth and named Haroldo[1] but started going by Holly and presenting herself as a woman after she left home. She became a prostitute in order to have enough money to eat. In the late sixties and early seventies she appeared in films and plays made by members of Andy Warhol's entourage, most notably starring in the films *Trash* and *Women in Revolt*, both directed by Paul Morrissey and produced by Andy Warhol. Woodlawn affirms the accuracy

---

[1]I'd like to point out that I am deadnaming certain trans people in this book—that is, referring to their birth name although they go by a different name since coming out—which should generally be avoided and is in many cases a form of transphobia and basic disrespect. I do this with some trepidation, but my purpose here is to give a quick glance at these people's life stories in order to provide context for the song in question. Normally I would contact the person to ask if they mind if I do this, but the people mentioned here are all dead.

of Reed's song: "I had $27, so I hitchhiked across the USA. I did pluck my eyebrows in Georgia. It hurt!"[2]

Candy Darling: Though born in Queens, Candy came from out on the Island, specifically Massapequa, Long Island, where she spent most of her childhood. She grew up as a boy by the name of James Slattery, but considered herself a woman from the time she was a teenager, wearing makeup and dresses and frequenting gay bars. She came to New York in the early sixties and befriended Holly Woodlawn and Jackie Curtis—the three of them saw themselves as a glamorous trio. She appeared briefly in the 1968 Warhol film *Flesh*, and starred in 1971's *Women in Revolt*. In 1969 the Velvet Underground opened their third album with "Candy Says," a Lou Reed song about Darling. She went on to appear in plays and independent films until her death in 1974, caused by lymphoma.

Little Joe: Joe Dallesandro was born to a 16-year-old mother in Pensacola, Florida. When Joe was five years old, his mother was sentenced to five years in federal prison for interstate auto theft, and his father brought him to New York City and placed him in foster care. He worked as a nude model starting at the age of seventeen. He met Andy Warhol and Paul Morrissey in 1967 when they were shooting *Four Stars*. They cast him in the film on the spot when they met him, after which he became a recurring star in Warhol's films. He went on to considerable success acting in mainstream films.

---

[2]Dave Simpson, "Bet You Think This Song Is About You," *The Guardian*, December 12, 2008.

His is the crotch pictured on the cover of the Rolling Stones' *Sticky Fingers* album, and he's also the shirtless model on the cover of the Smiths' debut LP.

Sugar Plum Fairy: This may refer to actor Joe Campbell, who starred as a gay prostitute named Sugar Plum Fairy in Andy Warhol's 1965 film *My Hustler*. But according to Warhol collaborator Billy Name, "If you're in the world of music or drugs, there is always a Sugar Plum Fairy. The one who delivers, or brings the stuff to you. Now, during this time from '64 to '70, there were two individuals I knew who were called the Sugar Plum Fairy as a nickname. Neither of the individuals who were the Sugar Plum Fairy were important to remember. Their only significance was that they became that character at that point. Lou, in 'Walk on the Wild Side,' took poetic license: *the* Sugar Plum Fairy, *the* Man, like in. . . . 'I'm Waiting For the Man.' The guy who delivers to you. The Sugar Plum Fairy."[3]

Jackie Curtis: Born in New York City and originally named John Curtis Holder, Jr., Jackie dressed at different times as a man and a woman, and often performed as a drag queen. She appeared in a few Warhol films, and wrote and starred in a number of plays. She was an amphetamine (speed) addict—hence the line, "Jackie was just speedin' away"—and later became a heroin addict, leading to her death from an overdose in 1985, aged 38. Friend Jayne County corroborates Lou Reed's lyric: "Jackie was a drag queen. She also had an identity crisis where she thought she was James Dean. She

---

[3] *Walk On the Wild Side.* Directed by Stephane Sendaoui. United States, 2005.

thought James Dean's spirit had come back and possessed her body. But I can't imagine James Dean's spirit coming back and taking possession of a drag queen's body. I don't think he'd do that. Do you?"[4]

*   *   *

Herbie Flowers, the bassist on "Walk on the Wild Side," was paid by the instrument. Which is to say, if he played two instruments on a session, he made double what he would have made if he only played one of them, regardless of hours spent in the studio. This, by his own admission,[5] is why he chose to play two bass lines dubbed over each other, one on upright acoustic bass and one on electric bass. I don't deny that.

But those bass lines, probably the most recognizable musical hook in all of Lou Reed's recorded work, have more behind them than that. These dueling bass parts set the mood instantly and fully. We move back and forth between the chords C and F, the electric bass ascending to the third of the F while the acoustic bass descends to the root of that chord a few octaves down. Then they move back toward each other to land on the home C chord again. Away from each other, back toward each other, and away again, a flirtatious dance. These choices aren't accidental; the song is flirting with us. Flowers's technique of sliding between notes also mirrors Lou Reed's cultural and emotional ambiguities: we're going back and forth fluidly and playfully between two modes of being. A slide indicates a subtlety of transition, which is

[4]Ibid.
[5]Herbie Flowers, "Playing Second Fiddle," BBC Radio 4, July 2005.

perfect for "Wild Side," because the song's whole goal is to tell us how easy it is to try something we've never tried before, whether it be a non-heteronormative sexual experience or buying a Lou Reed record. Slide on over here, honey.

*   *   *

This song is not the best song on the album; it *is* the album. It's a perfect encapsulation of both the album's overarching mood and its central cultural stance. When you are thinking of *Transformer* you are thinking of this song. All the other songs take place on the Lower East Side block that this song describes, and the Central Park of "Perfect Day" or the Times Square of "I'm So Free" are only peripheral attachments to that stretch of let's say Delancey Street that is the real center of the real city. This is where the action is. "Vicious" may be track one, but this is the first song on the record, the doorway to its world. As the first Lou Reed song most people hear, it's an invitation into his kingdom, finally aimed through the radio at everyone.

In a striking departure from his usual antisocial grouchiness, Reed actually sounds *inviting*. He invites us, if we're curious, to enter a place we've never been before. "Take a walk," it says, spend just one night in my kingdom; then you can go back to your bourgeois comfort, or your Simon & Garfunkel and Grand Funk Railroad and Beatles. The title phrase is spoken in character—this is something Candy or Joe said to a passerby—I picture a clean-cut fratboy slumming it for a couple hours in downtown Manhattan on a Friday night and feeling a movement between his legs when he hears the husky voice coming from a stubbly lipsticked mouth—but also of course we hear the real Lou Reed saying it to us, a queer seducing the straight world and forever destabilizing it, leaving it with an experience of hitherto unknown sexual and socioeconomic realities it can never fully forget.

Yes, this is Lou's commercial breakthrough and a relative creative breakthrough as well, because he's learned a way to let himself stop saying "fuck off" and start saying, "come in, come here, let me show you something." The title phrase vocalizes the deceptive quality of the whole record, its innocuous invitation to try out something else, just for tonight, just for half an hour, not letting on that you may be forever changed. No big deal, it says, as do all the songs on the album. Just a walk on the wild side. Just a perfect day. Just a New York conversation. It's all a laugh, give it a try, what's the big issue?

Reed's always been capable of speaking in this register. The Velvet Underground was the perfect band name because of this sly come-hither, implying that the underside of the city could beckon us like a soft plush boudoir. "It's nothing at all," assured the first song on their first record. But it wasn't until *Transformer* that what the mainstream could swallow at last matched up with Lou's capacity to sugar-coat his poison. Gone, for the moment, is the grandiose driving toward death of "Heroin," another song where he tells us to "take a walk" ("all you sweet girls with all your sweet talk"), but with the opposite meaning: "get away from me" was the central, or anyway the loudest, message of the Velvet Underground. At their most fearsome, the Velvets sounded like they didn't want you as a fan; they made that clear with their frightening feedback and alienating subject matter. But they always tempered it with a dose of pop, a welcoming melody here, a hook there.

Back then, the dose was too small to win over many pop fans. Now, on *Transformer*, Reed's perfected a ratio of these two co-dependent tones of voice that will take him from cult hero to international icon. For this record, with "Wild Side" at its core, the "come closer and see" attitude is the main ingredient, and the antisocial fury is peppered in only occasionally. Notably, however, he never stops saying "get away" as his career goes on. He continues to play "Heroin," makes both *Metal Machine Music* and *Coney Island Baby*. He pushes us away and pulls us in, and in so doing allows the idea of uncompromising arty pop music, a contradiction in terms, to exist.

This paradox is also a quintessential element of twentieth-century queer progress. Part of why this song is a classic is because it's a pop music microcosm of queers entering the mainstream consciousness, with all the simultaneous friendliness and condescending hostility that that process has entailed. The song manages to sustain both of those attitudes throughout—in fact, I hear them both fully expressed in the quick, innocuous phrase: "hey, babe."

Of course it's a friendly phrase. It's more than friendly; it's a sexual advance. But it's a condescension as well. And because it's a nickname usually used by men to address women, especially strangers on a city street, the "hey babe" becomes a feminization of the male passerby, and therefore a way of diminishing him, which ultimately reveals the hostility in the phrase. We can feel its sarcasm in the way Lou delivers it. From a disenfranchised queer to a straight man—a member of the ruling class that has declared his sexuality a crime and pushed him and all his queer friends into an underworld of

New York squalor—the word "babe" can only be said with a brutally ironic edge.

In "Walk on the Wild Side," Reed perfectly mirrored the LGBT world's in-progress appeal to heterosexual society. As gay and transgender people affirmed their identities and began to insist that they be treated decently, Lou Reed made his own presence known in pop culture by telling his queer friends' stories, saying their names, seeing them, and allowing a new audience to see them. He succinctly evokes the under-represented charms of gay life in mid-century New York without editing out the hitchhiking, prostitution, and drug addiction that went with it. The song's great victory, an enormous step forward both for Reed's career and for pop culture as a whole, is that it allowed authentically queer figures to show up on the radio.

When trying to productively confront a large population with something they have hated and feared in the past, as was the task of the gay rights movement (and Lou Reed's small role in it), marginalized people have various options of how to make their approach. These fall into three overarching categories. One can

a. be friendly, assuring people that this unfamiliar idea is not as scary as it seems

b. get angry, strategically attacking and disrupting the society that has abused you, or

c. ignore reactions, being true to oneself and letting the chips fall where they may.

These categories could equally apply to someone coming out to their friends and family, negotiating how to show up as a queer in the hallways of their school or workplace. All three of them are part of the ongoing struggle, small- and large scale, for gay rights. And all three of them show up in the song "Walk On the Wild Side." The song is, simultaneously:

a. a sincere and friendly invitation to uninformed straight folks to think about queers as real people for the first time

b. a pissed-off, sarcastic response to widespread heterosexual condescension to queers (plus, as the first Top 40 hit to reference prostitution, transsexuals, oral sex, and amphetamines, it was certainly an act of aggression), and

c. a simple and truthful set of stories about people Lou Reed actually knew, that is, an authentic expression of a queer culture that manages to sound like it truly doesn't care what the straight world thinks of it.

However you feel about and act toward the straight world, if you're queer, this song probably contains some of that feeling and stance. Not an easy thing to pull off as a songwriter. And Lou, damn him, sounds like he's barely even trying, shuffling casually between two guitar chords and talk-singing the lyrics, his vocal affect never rising.

This is where Lou Reed's sedate delivery, which on *Transformer* is more bored-sounding than any of his previous recordings, becomes a source of great power. The message of the song is this: these people that you've feared or fetishized are just people. It's really not such a big deal; it's just people trying to live their lives. Lou's bored voice and the laid-back band underscore this perspective. To Lou, it's so unremarkable that it's almost not worth singing about, except that most pop music fans don't know much about these kinds of people. "I always thought it would be kinda fun to introduce people to characters they maybe hadn't met before," he once said in reference to this song, "or hadn't wanted to meet."[6]

It's important that "Wild Side" introduces us to queer people's stories and doesn't much comment. That's sort of Lou's trademark: that he withholds judgment, giving the impression of an objective observer, a reporter. Thus he can talk about people he finds interesting and actually do their stories justice, as opposed to moralizing about them. Bob Dylan—an early inspiration to Reed—is usually judging his characters ("Like A Rolling Stone") or worshipping them ("Sad Eyed Lady of the Lowlands"). In his best work, Lou never does either. He tells their story in a few lines. This is supposed to be an amoral act, and it is, but it functions as a sign of respect. Withholding comment makes space for someone's story to speak for itself and spares it the withering, shrinking effect of passing judgment, positive or negative. The less you say about it, the more the story can contain.

This landmark song, calmly and organically, both exemplifies the queer confrontation of the straight

[6]Bockris, *Transformer*, 207.

mainstream and acts as Lou Reed's first address to the commercial mainstream, as though they were the same act, the same confrontation. Which, for this particular artist at this particular moment, maybe they are.

* * *

Lou Reed, of course, can't just write a great song with a progressive perspective. He's a true New York punk, and, like it or not, he's going to do something tactless and antisocial. So there's no way out of this chapter without addressing the matter of the colored girls.

First of all, the girls actually singing on this track are not, in fact, colored. They are a white British vocal trio called the Thunderthighs. So if you want to view it unforgivingly, both Reed and Bowie are using black women as a token signifier while also failing to employ any black women. Not a good look, protest all you like about how "colored" was common and inoffensive parlance for most of Lou Reed's life up to that point.

Referring to non-white people as "colored" was rather recently outdated in 1972; it went out after the civil rights movement ended state-enforced segregation in the Southern United States. Some people would have found it offensive, others not, as indicated by the fact that RCA Records sent out an edited version to radio stations in which Reed instead sings "and the girls all say . . ." Some stations aired the edited version, others the original. Essentially, the phrase was safely risqué, kind of like saying "midget" or "cripple" today. Disrespectful, but most people won't call you on it. "Colored" is what Reed and most other people would have called black people less than a decade earlier—which is, of course, when the action of the song takes place, describing people who came into Andy Warhol's orbit in the mid-sixties. But it also expresses disregard for an oppressed group's preferred term.

If you have any doubt that Lou Reed is, to say the least, unconcerned with racial sensitivity, look up the lyrics to "I Wanna Be Black" (*Street Hassle*, 1977). That song makes more explicit the implicit unexamined racism already fully present in "Wild Side." Reed doesn't hate black people. Rather, he stereotypes and fetishizes them, which is in some ways a more insidious way of dehumanizing someone. I don't deny that Reed at times, probably most times, had plenty of respect for black people, had black friends who were actually his friends, and looked up to many black musicians as genuine personal heroes. As it turns out, none of that precludes you from being racist, saying racist things, disrespecting non-white people. Deep breaths, Lou Reed fans. Say it with me: "I Wanna Be Black" and "Walk on the Wild Side" are racist songs. They are instances of Lou Reed being racist.

The intended effect of the section of the song in question is to convey a bored sarcasm but also an affectionate homage. Lou loves, adores, the black singing groups, doo-wop and soul music in which you can hear this type of harmonized vocalization. It's the stuff that blew his mind when he was a teenager listening to the radio. But on *Transformer*, if Reed feels something, he's got to accompany it with the assertion that he feels nothing. So his love for black music comes with a sneer at black music, as well as the sense that he's utterly bored with conventions of pop/rock. This is what's supposed to happen in a pop song: the doo-wop vocals come in, we all know the drill. He'll do it, but he's not going to pretend it's exciting or new.

Clever, Lou. As a way of presenting a hook in a pop song, it's funny, it's smart, etc. And yet here, the colored girls are seen as a tool for white people to make their music more likeable. It may be a kind of a compliment—black women are great singers, they're there because they deserve to be, black music is the coolest—but even that compliment is a sign of their use as a token, a musical luxury item that white people can pay for.

Thus, blackness is gleefully appropriated, and Lou often gets a free pass because he's in on the joke. Personally, I don't think being in on the joke is any excuse for it. Yeah, he's my hero, but I'm not letting Lou Reed get away with any of his casual racism and misogyny. The way I see it, if you respect someone, you call them on their bullshit.

Side Break
Lou in the Closet/Transformer in Code

I've been trying to figure it out. Why does Lou Reed mean so much to some people? Why does he mean so much to me? What is it about this guy in particular, among all the troubled geniuses in history, that I feel the need to write a book about him? I love Nina Simone, Bruce Springsteen, and Stephin Merritt, too, but I don't have 40,000 words to say about them. There's something about the godfather of punk that especially mystifies me. I can't leave him alone.

One thing that may have intensified the problem is that I ended up meeting him. I had the strange privilege to perform two Lou Reed songs in front of Lou Reed himself, and exchange a few words with him afterwards. I was twenty-one years old and had recently formed a band called Ezra Furman & the Harpoons. In 2008 the four of us went down to Austin, Texas to play at the South-by-Southwest festival, an exhaustingly media-hyped and corporation-branded event intended for music industry professionals first, music fans second. Lou Reed was the keynote speaker that year, and a tribute covers show was being put together which Lou himself was supposed to close out. Our friend and manager knew one of the organizers of the event who, to our shock and delight, decided to put us on the bill.

The event was in a big dusty courtyard of the FADER fort, a building that was, at least that week, dedicated entirely to advertising denim and sunglasses, partly by giving them away to artists. We made out like bandits, being broke college students with holes in all our jeans. Still, the branded-ness of the place was disturbingly intense. They also gave everyone there unlimited free leading-brand alcohol. Everything was deeply un-punk. You had to wonder how this was supposed to be making reference to any idea of counter-culture or artistic integrity with a straight face.

We performed in the mid-afternoon, about halfway through the event, between Yo La Tengo and Mark Kozelek, who must have had more important things to do later in the day or they wouldn't have been on so early. Anyway, it was a good spot and we were incredibly nervous. We played "New Age" with the goal of sounding like the original recording, which I'm sure we didn't quite achieve. Then I took the stage alone and played "Heroin" on an acoustic guitar, a spastic version I'd been developing since I was fifteen. The drunk crowd loved both performances. I can't say I really even remember them. My head was spinning.

Out of the corner of my eye I saw Lou Reed at the side of the stage, among the fringe of the crowd, taking photographs. I found out later that he had become an amateur photographer and loved posting his photos on his website. You know, he studied journalism in undergrad at Syracuse. In his lifelong role as an observer, a chronicler of people around him, he briefly used me as a subject.

Looking back on this time in my life—after my fanboy heartbeat manages to calm down about The Legendary Lou Reed and all that—I'm amused, as are most thirty-year-olds at their twenty-one-year-old selves. I also look back with considerable estrangement. Though still getting paid to play music, I've changed in some noticeable ways. Most noticeable is the fact that I present my gender as much more feminine now than I did then. Though male, I wear dresses, makeup, pearls, tights. I am proudly and clearly queer. In 2008, however, I was spending all my time with uber-hetero indie rock dudes, wearing exactly what they wore and speaking exactly as they spoke. I was still trying to blend in with the hypermasculine way of being that all of my straight male friends and relatives exuded. I didn't have gay friends or gender–non-conforming friends. Though sexually active, I had never been physically involved with a man. My close friends knew I was bisexual, but that fact came up only very occasionally. Though "officially" out of the closet with regard to sexuality, I was as closeted as could be when it came to my actual everyday behavior.

Gender-wise, I was even more repressed. Masculinity felt like a prison to me, a set of rules that had always been rigidly required of me and with which I had almost never felt comfortable. Still, I played along with the bros—in fact I positively saturated myself in bro-ness—because that was more convenient, and I was and had always been a shy, conflict-averse kid. Though I was definitely queer, I didn't see myself as queer *enough* to merit the social disruption and enormous emotional effort it would take to assert myself as such.

Lou Reed and the Velvet Underground were the perfect counterpart to this flickering, uncertain identity. When I first heard them, they took hold of me immediately and deeply. At age fifteen, I was looking for useful role models and not finding many. But I found one in Lou Reed. Because he wasn't this or that. He didn't fit into categories familiar to me like hippie or punk, straight or gay. He was free.

Most people I knew back then who were into punk or indie music liked the Velvet Underground. They were legendary, an influence on practically every band that considered itself even mildly arty or alternative, so they were hard to miss if you learned any background about those bands. We used to park the car in a parking lot, roll up the windows, and listen to "Heroin" at top volume, getting off on the song's anarchic build and drive toward some kind of unknown freedom or destruction, an impulse we all possessed.

The argument I would always get into with the teenagers in my orbit who were into the Velvet Underground was: Which was their best album? The cool-kid answer was *The Velvet Underground & Nico*, or even, for the more serious non-conformist, *White Light/White Heat*. These, the Velvet Underground's first two records, were their noisier and artier efforts, when John Cale was still in the band and pushing them toward atonality and avant-garde drone. Their later albums, insisted the kids who were more "punk" than I was, were when they started making a clumsy attempt to create something radio-friendly, commercial. As much as the Velvets were the ultimate non-conformists, their artistic integrity unassailably pure, their later records were closer to sell-outs.

My answer to the question of the best Velvet Underground album was, by all my opinionated comrades' reckoning, objectively wrong. I preferred *Loaded,* their 1970 swan song. The hipper kids gently but firmly corrected me: That's barely a Velvet Underground album. Mo Tucker didn't play drums on it. Reed quit the band when it was halfway finished. Bassist Doug Yule sings half the songs. It was heavily edited by the record label to make it more commercial. Even the title refers to the label's deplorable request that they make an album "loaded with hits," an order with which the band meekly attempted to comply.

But none of that stuff matters, I told them. Listen to the *songs.* It's got the best songs of any Velvet Underground record, and nothing else matters.

I still might (*might*) argue that the songwriting is the strongest on the final VU record, but that's not the real reason I passionately defended *Loaded* as their best work. The real reason, as is typical of teenagers' opinions about pop culture, was that I was using music as a way to try to carve out a cultural identity for myself, to find a place to plant my flag. And I didn't want to put myself in the John Cale-idolizing, art-should-be-difficult-and-challenging camp, because that camp was full of people with facial piercings, T-shirts displaying song lyrics written in permanent marker, and colorfully dyed hair. In other words, that camp represented the people who were adopting the rules and signifiers of the subculture known as Punk. For all my love of punk records, I was not going to be a part of that subculture or any other. I could not declare myself as being unambiguously a part of anything that resembled a team. I wanted to float free of all of the categories and definitions that made up social life in high school. In my self-aggrandizing inner world, it was I who was the true non-conformist: the one who refused to conform to the restrictions to which the punks slavishly and seemingly unconsciously adhered.

As unhelpful as this theory of myself and surroundings turned out to be, I believe there was something similar going on in Lou Reed's mind when he decided to fire John Cale and make records that were (relatively) easier for the unhip everyman to like. Two albums into their career, the Velvet Underground had established a reputation as wildly innovative and difficult artistes who played louder and more abrasively than any band in the world. Reed as a songwriter had become notorious for his shocking lyrics about hard drugs and sadomasochism. In this context, he made possibly the boldest move he could make, which was to record a disarmingly gentle album of Tin Pan Alley–influenced folk-rock which included lilted lyrics like, "Jesus, help me find my proper place." This was titled simply *The Velvet Underground*, a subtly defiant suggestion that this band, having dropped the "*& Nico*" of their debut, was not what you thought they were. They were now stripped of accoutrement and in touch with their essential message; *this* sound was what the group was really about.

For me, this is the mode in which Lou Reed becomes most compelling as a personality. I trust an artist, and for that matter anyone at all, a lot more when they are not, down the line, exactly what one would expect them to be culturally. This signals that their behavior is not the dutiful embodiment of a preexisting cliché, but rather that it is likely to be coming from a place of authentic personal style or conviction. At age fifteen, when I heard these records, I was inwardly wriggling against the constraints of the preexisting cliché I was expected to perform: the successful heterosexual male. One could tell almost by just listening to his voice, and certainly if you did any research into his personal life, that the Lou Reed of the late sixties was wriggling as well.

Despite his being openly non-heterosexual, and broadcasting this fact loudly to the world in his songs and interviews, I feel a deep kinship to Lou Reed as a closeted queer. Sure, he had gay sex, and made no secret of it. But there are those of us who come out joyfully and obviously and full-heartedly, and then there are those of us who can't shake the habits of the closeted life, who will always fiercely guard our secrets and lie unnecessarily, because that's what we learned to do growing up. We may talk candidly about our sexuality, but we won't let anyone too close; we will always avoid confrontation and dodge the truth as knee-jerk reactions. I am, of course, talking about myself, but I sense the same dynamic at work in Lou, and that, more than anything, is why I can't stop listening to his records.

* * *

The closet is not necessarily as easy to get out of as it might seem. It begins with the verbal declaration to the world about your sexuality or gender. But after you've told people, you have to deal with their reactions, and your own intangible change in status. You've changed your public identity, and this will inevitably mess with your private identity. Now the two have mingled. You can't hug your secrets close in a private world anymore. Not all of them, anyway.

There are different ways to react to this. Some people feel a huge amount of relief, a joyfulness in honesty, free and easy about who they are, the burden lifted. For others, it doesn't feel like much has changed. I remember telling a couple of my closest pals I was bisexual by way of a dramatic email, feeling very vulnerable, like I might lose them as friends. They responded with easygoing supportiveness, along with a measure of confusion, as if to say, "Why did you think this would be a big deal? This doesn't change anything between us—of course it doesn't. We're your friends." I felt relieved at this, but I also felt a vague frustration. I wanted coming out to change something. I wanted them to understand the magnitude of the secrets I'd been keeping, the double life I felt I'd been living. I was like a child hiding from his parents, trying to scare them into thinking he had run away from home. Finally you come out of hiding hoping to provoke tears of relief, and your mother just says, "Oh, there you are. Dinner's almost ready."

As it turned out, I wasn't really out of the closet at all. I had more than just same-sex attraction to confess. I still didn't tell almost anyone about my habit of trying on the dresses of female acquaintances. I still felt caged in masculinity and afraid of being found out as "less of a man" than I was supposed to be. And then there was a general social dishonesty that may never fully leave me. Calling yourself bisexual doesn't do much by itself, and does not equal openness. It's a label, and as important as labels can be, wearing them is not equivalent to renouncing your duplicity, your feeling of being in hiding.

At some point, I had to adopt a deep change in attitude and start speaking inconvenient truths. And even so, I find myself returning again and again to the habit of hiding myself, imitating an ideal straight man I imagine straight people around me are more comfortable with. Maybe part of the reason I started wearing feminine clothes and accessories was in order to preclude the possibility of doing this. If you're wearing a dress it's going to be harder to transform into a straight-acting guy at the first sign of disapproval.

One of the things Lou Reed and I have in common is an eagerness to look to others for behavioral guidelines. This should not be confused with an eagerness to please. Though it sometimes does include that impulse, it encompasses more. You're hiding your real self—or, more frighteningly, you don't know if you even have a real self—so you become purely a reaction to other people. As he put it shortly after the release of his eponymous solo debut:

> I write through the eyes of somebody else. I'm always checking out people I know I'm going to write songs about. Then I become them. That's why when I'm not doing that, I'm kind of empty. I don't have a personality of my own. I just pick up other people's personalities. I mean seriously, if I'm around someone who has a gesture that's typical of them, if I'm around them for more than an hour, I'll start doing it. And if I really like it, I'll keep it until I meet someone else who has something else. But I don't have anything myself.[1]

[1] Bockris, *Transformer*, 203.

Surely this sheds light on Lou's elusiveness, why he's always been so difficult to categorize. It's painful to hear him say, "I don't have a personality of my own." It's clear to me that he's afraid—with good reason, by the way—that people will emotionally destroy him if he reveals his true personality.

This general social shiftiness is the root of his elusion of categories in his musical life. The world of pop culture needs categories, and record stores need genre headings to organize the racks of albums. But a real person is complicated and contains multitudes; sometimes so complicated that there's no clear digestible story that can be told about them. And anyway, they—we—don't owe you that. We don't owe you an unambiguous label.

Lou Reed is my hero for his uncontrollable multiplicity of selves. From him I got the message that you don't have to choose sides, you don't have to join a team, you don't have to give them a handy definition of yourself. That's also partly why, sexuality and clothing style aside, he's a perfect gay icon. Ambiguity is a major building block of queerness, and Lou Reed may be the most ambiguous rock star who ever lived. It's an inspiring "fuck you" to a world that would have preferred to categorize and tame him.

But equally important is the painful element of this existential stance. Lou doesn't want you to look at him for too long. His ventriloquism, his continual insistence on using his art to document people other than himself, is the kind of misdirection typical of someone trying to pass in a culture that wants their blood. No matter how proud I am of my various identities, I will always relate to the impulse to make myself invisible, even as I desperately try to grab people's attention and soak up their love. Reed was a gay Jew in an anti-Semitic and homophobic society. What could be a more useful defense than saying, "Nothing to see over here—hey, look at that strange person over there, isn't that interesting?"

* * *

As others have pointed out, rock 'n' roll derives a crucial energy from sexual repression. Codified as a distinct genre in the fifties, the music immediately caused alarm across conservative America, which made it all the more marketable to the rebellious teens of the baby boom. As sexually charged art gradually became more tenable as mass culture, pop music took on an increasingly vital excitement which, like a good orgasm, reached an ecstatic breaking point and then lost its driving tension.

By the early seventies, pop culture is in a state of postcoital numbness. Brazenly open acknowledgment of sexuality—at least heterosexuality—is now firmly entrenched as highly lucrative, conventional entertainment. When one can freely sing about sex and become a millionaire, the music loses the fraught, risky quality that was so appealing in, say, Little Richard's singles from the mid-fifties.

This vitality, this sense of repressed energies, pervades Lou Reed's music up to and including *Transformer*. Though he's known for being miles ahead of late-sixties sexual openness—"Venus in Furs" was recorded in 1966—we still feel, on *Transformer*, the energizing tension and pain of a sexuality straining against the bars that cage it.

After all, the sexual revolution, like everything else, mostly excluded non-heterosexuals. The barriers to Lou

Reed's freedom, and that of any queer person, were much larger than those faced by most straight people. Young people gradually grew unafraid to be sexual; as mass media haltingly broached the topic, it was discovered—big surprise—that most people didn't mind being entertained in more titillating ways than they'd been used to, leaving aside the old squares who weren't as commercially powerful as a target audience anyway. Being gay, however, was another story. It was illegal, dangerous, and socially unacceptable. Being into "free love," as a cultural stance, was utterly hip and life-affirming as long as you weren't a homo. If you were, you could lose your job, your housing, your friends.

Thus, Lou Reed in 1972 still had the risky sex-criminal status that the world of heterosexual rock 'n' roll had forever lost. Being in touch with a sexuality still considered deviant from mainstream culture gave him a sense of the mystery and danger that was missing from pop music as it slumped into the seventies. What's striking is how subtly he exploits it. Having earned a reputation as sexually deviant purveyor of "sleaze rock," one might expect Reed to beat it to death, writing to shock and titillate. Instead, he seems to do the opposite, burying his sexual energy in conventional rock lyrics that verge on blandness. Notwithstanding the notable exception, "Take A Walk On the Wild Side," the lyrics of *Transformer* tend to read, at first glance, as a collection of rock clichés, from romantic frustration ("you just keep me hanging on") to egomaniacal boasting ("I do what I want . . . I'm so free"), to prudish sexual jealousy ("I've been told that you've been bold with Harry, Mark and John"). Sure, there are a couple of odd lines—"You know what they say about honey bears"—but they don't sound like they're betraying anything truly countercultural. Lyrically, the album propping up the big transgressive hit ("Wild Side") doesn't seem particularly daring.

As it turns out, there's evidence that this was done intentionally, even acutely self-consciously. This record was very much designed to be his big commercial breakthrough, and to use one's underground, socially unacceptable reputation in order to reach a mass audience is a weird, delicate task. Said Reed around the time of the album's release: "There's two outright gay songs, from me to them, but they're carefully worded so the straights can miss out on the implications and enjoy them without being offended."

I love this line. This is a line that contains multitudes, betraying not only an attitude about entertaining a large audience, but an entire worldview. The world doesn't understand us, it says. They can listen in, but they'll never understand. If you're on my side, you get it. If you're the rest of these chumps, go ahead, buy a record, but fuck you.

However, it's not the outright gay songs that are carefully worded and intended to fly under the casual listener's radar, but the other songs. Reed could hardly have been referring to the album at its gayest, considering the clearly queer intentions of some of the tracks. It's hard to believe Reed thought many would "miss out on the implications" of "we're coming out, out of our closets" (the refrain from "Make Up"). "Shaved his legs and then he was a she," from the opening verse of "Wild Side," is similarly blatant.

The gay-themed songs are hiding in plain sight. Many listeners were amazed that the line "even when she was giving head" was not censored on UK radio stations; the censors were, reportedly, not familiar with the term. But listening forty-odd years later, with the shock value of sexual songs considerably if not totally dulled, the non-explicit lyrics are where the real intrigue lies. These songs fascinate, not for the excess and over-the-top deviance that was associated with Lou Reed in the sixties, but rather for their understatement, their partially submerged aggression, and the damaged personality they both mask and expose.

* * *

When asked in 1979 how he felt about growing up closeted, Reed did not equivocate. "I resent it," he said. "It was a very big drag. From age thirteen on I could have been having a ball and not even thought about this shit. What a waste of time. If the forbidden thing is love, you spend most of your time playing with hate. Who needs that? I feel I was gypped."[2]

When I was a teenager I was fantasizing about gay sex and listening to the Velvet Underground. At the same time, I was in an all-male Jewish youth group (we called it a "high school fraternity"), playing sports while bitterly lamenting my lack of athletic ability, and memorizing Eminem's homophobic rap lyrics. Clearly, I was experiencing some significant cognitive dissonance. Like a lot of sixteen-year-olds, I was trying on a few different identities, hoping for one to lead me somewhere that made me feel better, able to imagine a future for myself.

[2]Ibid., 22–23.

This was the psychic landscape into which the Velvet Underground's eponymous third album gently slithered for the first time. Someone at school gave me a burned CD copy. I didn't expect it to be a revelation; I just expected it to be another great album from a great band. It turned out to be as much of a game-changer for my inner life as my initial discovery of the band had been.

The version of the album I had was not the most widely available version, but the less-common version known as the Closet Mix. It seems that after the album was tracked and mixed, Lou Reed returned to the studio alone and remixed the whole thing, going as far as to replace the agreed-upon version of "Some Kinda Love" with an entirely different take. Guitarist Sterling Morrison, dismayed at Reed's egotistical act of betrayal, said the band sounded muffled, like it was recorded in a closet, giving the version its nickname. This was the mix initially released in the United States, with the previous version, mixed by Val Valentin, released in the United Kingdom. But the Closet Mix did not stay in print, and when the album was reissued in 1985, ceasing to be a hard-to-obtain rarity, it was the Valentin mix that they pressed and released.

Such complex intra-band dynamics point to the beginning of the end of the Velvet Underground, but it is the appearance of the word "closet" in connection with a secret revision of what was supposed to be a collaborative mixing process which fascinates me, even stirs something in me. Lou Reed was sneaky, secretive, underhanded. The Closet Mix features the lead vocals (mostly sung by Reed) at the front of the mix and more separated from the other elements of the tracks; the band seem further in the background. This ups the sense of conversational intimacy already present in the album. It feels less like the band was shoved in a coat room and more like Reed has pulled you into a small dark enclosure to tell you his secrets.

I was right there in the closet with him. I wondered, too: "What do you think I'd see / if I could walk away from me?"

Side Two

Sino Two

"Make Up"
Lou and Gender

Real gendered self-consciousness dawns on most boys somewhere around the time that puberty hits. Or it did for me. My instinct is that girls snap to it earlier. Little girls, after all, feel the effects of patriarchy and sexism almost as soon as they learn to talk, with every "girly" toy or fairy-tale character or self-presentation subtly positioned as less legitimate or powerful than what seems to be its equivalent in the boys' realm. From the moment they see their first Disney princess and sense that they are supposed to want to be that and nothing else, they are invited to doubt themselves. But it takes something as shatteringly embarrassing as the human body's first assertions of change and desire to wake us boys up to that fact we knew all along but never believed: that other people can see us. That anyone might be looking and wondering, or laughing, at any moment.

Eleven years old, sixth grade, I realized two devastating facts. One, that the popular boys were good at sports and I wasn't good at sports. Two, that I was attracted to the boys at least as much as I was the girls. Or, to state these two realizations as one, I realized that I was less masculine than my classmates. I wouldn't have put it in those terms. In fact, I wouldn't have put it any terms, because you couldn't have gotten me to talk about it if you had tortured me with a burning spear. But I knew that I had secrets that made me a freak, a loser, a fag, whatever charged bully-type word was being thrown around. There was basically one option: to become invisible.

At age eleven, this was really pretty bleak. But as you grow older, you find ways to assert yourself, to make your weirdnesses work for you. I didn't become popular, but I started listening to punk rock and not caring what anyone thought about me, or saying that I didn't care and hoping it would become true. That didn't mean I was going to come out of the closet. It meant that I found a way to be less obvious about the fact that I was trying to erase large parts of myself. If a guy never says a word and looks nervous, it's obvious he's got a secret. If he starts acting out and playing loud music, he's just one of those non-conformist types. I learned to hide the fact that I was hiding, which is something you learn pretty quick if you're really serious about never being found out.

I was dreaming of wearing women's clothing pretty young. Eleven or twelve. I pretended Green Day's "King For A Day" was a joke, but I knew it wasn't. I knew I was girly inside, and I wanted girliness to be a part of my life. My femininity, a femininity that the misogyny and homo-/transphobia of everyday life made clear was totally forbidden to me, demanded attention I refused to give it. I was too scared to even try it in secret until I was maybe seventeen, when I got a cool female friend to let me try on her dress and underwear. No photographs. Too risky. You get the idea. It's an old story, common to huge numbers of boys, men and trans women, and a sad one. I'm just glad I eventually found a world in which this part of me could be allowed to breathe.

Didn't really find that world, though, until nearly ten years later. Of course the first time I wore a dress in public was onstage. Of *course*. By age twenty-five I'd formed a reasonably successful indie rock band, and wearing a dress onstage is (was?) a trope of alternative, punk-y bands. David Bowie, New York Dolls, Nirvana. It's a gag. Maybe it's a political gag, or meant as a progressive protest, but to most audience members it's just funny, or at best *fun*. I knew I could get away with it and no one would ask me if it had anything to do with who I actually was. And no one did. But I asked myself, and the locked doors in my head were starting to open.

I was dressed femme on a record cover before I had ever dressed femme around my friends. *Day of the Dog* (2013), plus the 7" sleeve for our single "My Zero." It gave me courage. I wore dresses onstage, then all day the day of the show, then on days I didn't have a show. I got into makeup, clumsily, painfully. I got some fake pearl necklaces and they became symbolic talismans of femininity that I clung to fiercely.

The voice of the transphobic mainstream is always just around a corner of your mind when you're striving toward a more authentic gender. It's saying, *You look ridiculous. You look ugly. Go home and change, now. You look like a monster.* Buying clothes is an emotional labyrinth full of trap doors that lead to the worst you've ever felt about yourself. You read about the rape and murder of transgender people and wonder how safe you'll ever really feel. And strangers on the street say things to you that you wish you could un-hear.

So when I hear my hero sing, dripping with pity and irony, "You're a slick little girl," well, I just have to wonder.

Are you turning on me, Lou?
Were we ever on the same side?
Are there sides?

* * *

Shortly after the dissolution of the Velvet Underground, Andy Warhol proposed that Lou Reed write songs for a Broadway musical he was devising, a collaborative project with fashion designer Yves St. Laurent. As mentioned previously, "Vicious" was originally an assignment to Reed for this potential collaboration as well. The thing didn't pan out, but it gave us our opening track and also got Reed writing showtunes like "New York Telephone Conversation," "Goodnight Ladies," and "Make Up." Withheld for the first half of *Transformer*, the cabaret/Broadway-style songs take up more than half of side B. Reed now reveals that in addition to sounding tough, he can perform full-on theatrical camp—a classic mode for the stereotype of an effeminate gay man.

Nevertheless, "Make Up" starts out in the closet, concealing its hand. He could be singing about a cis-gendered woman, if you haven't been listening too close. Why wouldn't he be? But if you've been paying attention, the album's trained you by now to assume queerness as surreptitiously ever-present; you know not to trust the surface appearance. The chorus, of course, comes out and says it: "We're coming out / Out of our closets." It's clear, then, that the verses describe a drag queen or transgender woman getting ready in the morning.

The harder-to-answer question is not the sex of the object of the lyrics, but how the singer sees that person. Before the chorus, you might mistake the mood for one of playful affection. But the opening lines suggest, on the contrary, a biting sarcasm to all of the subsequent adoration. "Your face when sleeping is sublime / But then you open up your eyes / Then comes pancake factor number one. . . ." The artifice of the person's public life ruins a natural, non-constructed beauty. A charged idea for Lou Reed as he remakes himself as a glam rocker. His self-defensive instinct is to mock the most stereotypical extreme of what he himself now is: a male-bodied person wearing makeup. "Perfume and kisses, ooh! it's all so nice," he jeers. Listening as a feminine-presenting man, it's hard to take these verses as any kind of show of solidarity with gender–non-conforming people. At best, he sees wearing makeup as a game, a childish diversion for a "little girl." At worst, he's disgusted and embarrassed by the drag queen he's singing about.

But then there's a sudden key change and he's spouting early-seventies gay rights slogans: "We're coming out, out of our closets, out on the streets." For me, it's painful to listen to. Clearly, he's trying to join the movement, he's trying to affirm the gay pride parades that march past his Manhattan apartment. But of course he can't just write a fist-pumping gay anthem; it has to include arch irony, bitter refusal to celebrate, poison fed to the people who think he's on their side. He can't honestly wave the flag of pride without also waving the flag of self-hatred. He is two-hearted, ambiguous, to the core.

The transphobia folded covertly into this song is, sadly, very much reflective of its era. To join the gay rights movement in the early seventies, one had to deal with the inconvenient reality of transgender people. Trans women were particularly inconvenient. Part of gay liberation's intention was to convince the straight world that gay men were in fact "real men," that they could be masculine and thus, in the prevailing misogynist worldview, legitimate. In the rush to align themselves with the heterosexual ruling class, gay activists were quick to distance themselves from trans people, who were deemed an embarrassment and hindrance to a movement whose success was highly dependent on how it looked to mainstream media. As Lou Reed's gay pride song, "Make Up" mirrors this dynamic by joining proud sloganeering with a palpable disdain for the feminine.

Not that the song isn't doing something important here. Positioned at the top of Side Two, "Make Up" is making sure we are 100 percent aware that this is a gay album. If the effeminacy of "Vicious" was drowned out by the cock-rock backing band, if you missed that Holly and Candy were not designated female at birth, here's a song that shoves it in your face as soon as you flip the record: we're coming out, Lou declares as the drums and guitar drop out. Out of our closets. Am I being crystal clear, here?

But, as with the gay rights movement's erasure of trans people, it's when you have to simplify yourself to be understood that you often end up erasing the subtleties that make you human. This dynamic may be what characterizes *Transformer* more than any other single element: Lou is trying to translate himself to a huge audience, and in the process he makes himself into a cartoon. Ultimately, this is what allows him to become an icon. But what gets repressed in the process, Reed's inconvenient multivalencies, always find a way to show themselves. They're always there, lurking for the listener who wants them, who feels their muffled urgency too.

For example, this song contains what for me are the saddest lines on the album, a broken heart only partly obscured by the sarcasm. "When you're in bed it's so wonderful / It'd be so nice to fall in love / When you get dressed I really get my fill / People say that it's impossible." The speaker still has a dream of a real healthy relationship with his made-up male-bodied lover, but the world won't allow it, the speaker himself can't bring himself to allow it. The impossibility of love is the foundation of his hatred. It's awful, and I relate.

This is almost surely a projection of my own experience, but I can't help myself: I sense shades of gender dysphoria running deep in the thirty-year-old Lou Reed. It would be hard to argue that he secretly saw himself as a woman or even as genderless or otherwise non-binary; there's just not much evidence pointing to that, notwithstanding his intermittent aura of androgyny. But I believe that the binary system of gender—the idea that one must be either male or female, and that certain social roles and mores go along with those categories—constrict all of us to different degrees. Someone like me, who often has felt suffocated by a pressure to look and behave in accordance with widely held concepts of masculinity, is further toward the dysphoric end of the scale than someone who once in a while is annoyed that he is expected, for instance, to be good with power tools. Someone who feels so at odds with the gender they were assigned at birth that they are suicidal, on the other hand, is further along the dysphoria scale than I am, and would probably benefit enormously (as I have) from a change in gender presentation.

I have to wonder, where would Lou Reed place himself on this scale? He tends to downplay any element of identity when talking about his gender subversion. "Guys walking around in makeup is just fun," he told Lester Bangs in 1973. "Why shouldn't men be able to put on makeup and have fun like women have?"[1]

But for some men—or people who have been called men but don't consider themselves men—it's not "just fun," but an act of self-preservation. Is Lou Reed one of those people, or is he just having a good time giving the middle finger to gender norms? How high are the stakes of his breaking of male taboos?

If you think he's going to tell you, you're crazy.

[1]Lester Bangs, "Lou Reed: A Deaf-Mute in a Telephone Booth," *Let it Rock*, November 1973.

"Satellite of Love"
Lou and Pop

Lou Reed is a control freak. Blame it on electroshock therapy, blame it on Andy Warhol, blame it on an inborn lust for power; it doesn't matter. Control matters more to him than anything. And you don't want to work with a control freak. Lou Reed will collaborate with you, but the better the collaboration works out, the more he will see you as a threat. Then he will get rid of you. It happened to John Cale, Andy Warhol, Velvet Underground manager Steve Sesnick, and finally David Bowie. He needs to work with other people to be successful—his greatest moments are a result of finding the right collaborator, as Cale and Bowie prove—but if you're good enough to have a positive influence on the project, it will result in your being fired. Because it's his project. Because nobody tells Lou Reed what to do.

But perhaps even he recognized that he went a little too far in firing the entire Velvet Underground. Just before he self-righteously left the band, he had been inches from the stardom he'd craved for years. After a soul-searching exile on Long Island, he returns in 1972, and he's got another chance. Which is why it's possible to see *Transformer* as a kind of remake of the final Velvet Underground album, *Loaded*. It, too, is designed to be "loaded with hits," and if he has to give a little control over to Bowie, fine, he'll grit his teeth and let the thing get away from him a little, creatively and aesthetically, so he can be sure it'll be a blockbuster. Just as he hoped, he becomes a star. (Of course, having ceded as much control as he could bear for as long as he could stand, he never works with Bowie again and their friendship utterly deteriorates in the ensuing years.)

Going into the studio with Bowie, Lou brings the most radio-friendly songs he's got.[1] He had demoed a surefire single for *Loaded* called "Satellite of Love" that would have fit that album quite nicely, and which the Velvets pulled off well. I suspect it felt a little *too* commercial, even for *Loaded*. Doug Yule describes hearing about it for the first time in 1970 while the Velvets were still together: "I remember riding in the back of a taxi or a limo with Lou and Steve [Sesnick] and Steve kind of going on about, oh, we've gotta get some airplay, and Lou saying oh, I've got this song called 'Satellite of Love,' cause some satellite was up at that point and it was a big deal, the space race was going on. And Steve saying, yeah, that'll do it. It was kind of a constant thing about airplay, being more commercial, being more accepted in the FM world."[2]

Funny enough, David Bowie, who in 1970 Lou hadn't yet met, had pulled this off with "Space Oddity" the year before,

---

[1] Richard Robinson, on "Walk on the Wild Side": "I honestly don't know why we didn't record it [for *Lou Reed*]. He may have been holding onto it—for something better." He also was toying with "Satellite of Love" during the *Lou Reed* sessions, but decided against recording it. David Fricke, "Metamorphosis," *Mojo*, November 2016, 75.

[2] "The Velvet Underground—Doug Yule Part 7." YouTube video, 5:50. Posted by "prismfilms1," uploaded January 27, 2014. https://www.youtube.com/watch?v=Gcyx25T-NRc.

capitalizing on an international pop culture event by recording a song for the occasion. Lou may have heard it and cockily thought, "I could write a better outer-space song than *that*."

Even without the "Space Oddity" parallel, you can tell it was written for the FM world for two reasons: (1) musically, it's unusually cheerful for Lou Reed; it's fun, it's got an optimistically rising bass line, it could be on the radio and (2) It's close to meaningless; it's about nothing. But no one writes about Nothing (or "Nuthin'") quite like Lou.

Let's talk about (1) first. There's actually musical *lift* here, a joyful ascent, which is a rare mode for Reed. His three go-to musical moods are tough boredom, simmering tension, and full-on assault. This one's opening chord progression, via a subtle change from the major second chord to a minor second and then to the fifth, seems to continually rise even when it returns to its home chord. By the song's coda, which progressively builds as more musicians join in (horns and backing vocals, then more backing vocals, then more horns), we're practically in "Hey Jude" territory in terms of sheer musical joy. "Satellite" has something in common with Bowie's "Changes" as well; listen to the songs side by side and you can hear Reed and Bowie trying to launch themselves to the top of the charts through sheer chordal upthrust. Hard to know which of the two artists pushed for this song to be recorded, but Bowie had to be a motivating factor, having broken through with orbit-obsessed material like "Space Oddity" and "Starman."

But where Bowie is inside the spacecraft or making contact with celestial beings, Reed is half-interestedly watching the footage on television. Pre-stardom, he's afraid of being left behind—he knows he's as good as any of the best pop stars of the sixties, but he's been snubbed. He sees himself as having been too progressive, too uncompromising, for his own good. "Heroin" and "White Light/White Heat" are not songs likely to make one rich. *Transformer* is his last-ditch Hail Mary attempt to transcend what holds him back, and "Satellite" is as far from his unvarnished, avant-garde, aggressive self as he's gotten yet.

The question is, does he really even *want* to ascend? Does he want orbit, does he want fame, or would he rather stay home and watch it on TV, saying "that could have been me?" Next to Bowie, Lou does seem highly earthbound, not built for the pop stratosphere. It's fascinating to hear Bowie's vocals alongside Lou's on this track. Reed's voice—here and pretty much throughout this album—stays firmly in an apathetic lower register, while Bowie belts out the angelic high parts, trying to lift his low-energy hero, finally giving up on him and soaring to the top of the scale in the exultant outro. The result is a song that works better than most tracks by either of the artists on their own: where Bowie would tend to drift, unmoored, out into inhuman celebrity persona, Lou tethers him to a New York City living room. Where Reed, left to his own devices, might wallow in the drone of his own bored machismo, Bowie provides a buoyant spirit of extroverted adventure. The sense of fighting gravity allows the song to do what pop music does best: struggle, make a mighty push to shed what holds it back.

The struggle is all Reed's, all internal. Is this the moment of transcendence that has eluded him, where he finally connects with the world at large? Or is this where he crashes down to earth, giving up on his sixties dream of being a true artist, and becomes a pop music shill like the ones he and his fans have always disdained?

The answer could depend on whether you think the best version of Lou Reed is the one who becomes a twisted version of a superstar, or the one that folds his arms and says "fuck you" to the mainstream. Or the answer could be simply, complexly, "both." He is both a star and an anti-star, and this song is both a triumph and a failure. A triumph in accessibility, craft, and sheer pleasure. A failure to remain the difficult and anti-commercial artist exemplified by works like "Sister Ray." In any case, it is a transformation, and one that never fully resolves or finishes. He may be in orbit now, but he'll skid back into the gutter and the avant-garde time and again throughout his wonderfully, frustratingly various career.

* * *

It's kind of amazing how unmoved Lou Reed can sound while singing over some of the most bombastic and upbeat instrumentation of his career. It's partly his vocal range: by 1972, he's either incapable of or uninterested in singing higher than the point halfway up a piano's keyboard. But it's even more so his lyrics. Reed may claim the song is about jealousy, but the thing you really feel emanating from the singer is boredom.[3] The original Velvet Underground demo begins, in the light-hearted introductory manner of a Cole

---

[3]Reed, twenty-five years on: "I found sometimes you don't know what a song is about until years and years later. . . . I never realized just how much 'Satellite of Love' was about jealousy." Marlene Goldman, "Q&A: Lou Reed," *Rolling Stone* magazine, April 29, 1998. But even if the song is partly about jealousy, the boredom mostly drowns that aspect out. The short bridge about an unfaithful lover is inconsequential in the face of the larger message that Lou couldn't care less about anything. He doesn't react to the fact that he's

Porter tune: "In this world as we know it / Sorrows come and go / But now we see the human race / Has put its footprints on the moon's face." He's present for a monumental event in human history, and how does he feel about it? "I watched it for a little while. I like to watch things on TV."

The underlying parallel is to how he feels about this sea change moment in his career: working with David Bowie, poised to blow a hole in the Billboard charts, he can't help but feel underwhelmed, or at best mildly amused. He is passive, watching without comment, a pop culture consumer like any average American. He sounds lobotomized, and I think that's his intention.

Self-erasure: that is the goal of this song, as of so many pop songs. Lou Reed is a complicated person, and he knows complicated doesn't sell records. Simple sells records. Yes, he can write "The Black Angel's Death Song," a rapid-fire volley of cryptic fragments of half-spoken poetry which was known to clear Greenwich Village's Cafe Bizarre of its clientele in 1965, or "Lady Godiva's Operation," an unsettling account of a lobotomy gone wrong, set forth in vivid detail. These songs attack their audience and give the sense of unfiltered access to Reed's unusual mind. "Satellite," on the other hand, is what happens after the lobotomist's knife has been turned on Reed himself: he sits around watching TV and makes hit records. It's a great, uncomplicated pop song. But if you know its author's previous body of work, you know how much he's hiding.

been told that his lover has "been bold with Harry, Mark and John." He just repeats it and moves on, utterly detached.

"Wagon Wheel"
Lou and Laziness

This is where I start to feel a little embarrassed that I'm writing a book about *Transformer*. A song like "Wagon Wheel" doesn't exist to be analyzed. It's just a good band doing their thing. You can dance to it, you can get off on it, if you like rock 'n' roll. Why would you publish a study of a rock record? It's simple stuff. It's a few chords and a beat. It's dumb; that's what makes it good.

On the other hand: "I wanna write a Hamlet or a King Lear," says Lou. "My ambitions are very large. And my talent is large enough to handle them, I think."[1] This is from a 1982 interview, and is not an anomalous quote; Reed was known to compare himself to giants of literature. His dream was to be a great writer, and at many points he achieved that. Though I don't think he's quite Shakespeare, nor do I want him to be, I have no doubts about the fact that Reed is one of the best songwriters the world has seen, and that he upped the intellectual stakes of the entire endeavor.

[1]"Lou Reed Interview." YouTube video, 6:40. Posted by "Richard Pink," uploaded September 25, 2014. https://www.youtube.com/watch?v=OwzbfjrydXg.

Nevertheless: "Wagon Wheel." Truly a dumb song. Everyone's allowed a little filler, I suppose. But the writerly complacency of this song can be found in a lot of places throughout *Transformer*. Really, it's an arrogance: that Lou Reed can fart out a basic rock 'n' roll song and it'll still be better than 90 percent of contemporary pop music. He all but admits that this is what he's doing in this song's lyrics: "You've got to live your life as though you're number one." He's become a diva even before he's had a hit record. It's intentional: he espouses it here as a personal ethos. He's not number one, but he's living as though he is, which is kind of an irritating way to be. He was in the Velvet Underground and he hangs out with David Bowie, so he thinks he's hot shit. The frustrating part of trying to call him on this is, I tend to think he's just about as great as he thinks he is. Not only that, but it worked: thinking of himself as a star led to him becoming a star. Which, talent-wise, he deserved.

But still, come on. What is this song supposed to be about? "Be my wagon wheel?" He's just not trying, and it's frustrating. And his misogyny is back on display: "Just kick her in the head and rearrange her." Real nice. This is what Lou Reed does to you. Just when you've fallen in love with him, he reminds you that he's a total asshole.

The only place I can find that contains a hint of real content is the bridge, when the band shuts up for a second to let Lou briefly get faux-earnest: "Oh, Heavenly Father, what can I do? / What she's done to me / it's making me crazy. / Oh, Heavenly Father, I know I have sinned / But look where I've been / It's making me lazy." Here we may find, still audible through the obviously insincere Christian prayer mode, the heart of what this song is about. It's a lazily written song that is about laziness itself.

First of all, of course, rhyming "crazy" and "lazy" is just about the laziest thing a songwriter can do. There's just no good reason for Reed to use both words other than the fact that they rhyme. But it does hint at how he views his vocation as a songwriter. It's not the first time he's called himself lazy: in the first draft of the song "Ocean" (recorded at least twice, brilliantly, with the Velvet Underground before being released in much inferior condition on his 1972 solo debut) he tells us, "I am a lazy son / I never get things done / It really drives me crazy." The lazy-crazy pair is employed here as well, but so lazily that the words don't even end up rhythmically matching up enough to rhyme.

And yet, I can feel the emotional specter of his teenage post-electroshock fugue state in these lines, when he suffered from short-term memory loss and a reduced attention span. Despite the sarcasm of "Heavenly Father, I know I have sinned," Lou does indeed seem to be asking for forgiveness. *Look where I've been.* If you were a great writer who couldn't concentrate long enough to read a novel, you'd write simple three-minute songs too. *It's making me lazy.*

The song ends with the repeated plea, "Please don't let me sleep too long." He's asking for help, though he's not sure from whom. He's begging for transformation, to be somehow saved from his own lazy inertia.

* * *

In 1990, Lou Reed and John Cale released *Songs for Drella*, their first collaborative effort since Cale was fired from the Velvet Underground. The brilliant and strange fifteen-song LP is made up of songs written about Andy Warhol, who had died unexpectedly in 1987 at the age of 58. It is a loving tribute that avoids cheap sentimentality by honestly exploring both songwriters' complicated relationship with the pop art legend. One of the most revealing songs is called "Work," written and sung by Reed. Over frantic, repetitive distorted electric guitar and piano, Reed describes Warhol as productivity obsessed, with a work ethic baked into him by his Catholic upbringing. The song's refrain goes, "It's work. All that matters is work."

Warhol was known for this: he conceived of the act of making art as participation in the capitalist enterprise. His Factory was not named ironically; its purpose was to employ many workers to create a huge volume of saleable artworks. Lou learned from Andy to see music-making in the same way. "No matter what I did it never seemed enough," he sings in "Work." "He said I was lazy / I said I was young / How many songs did you write? / I'd written zero; I lied and said ten / You won't be young forever / You should have written fifteen / It's work!"

Knowing that his mentor vehemently encouraged him to focus on quantity at least as much as quality, one can better understand the ethos behind filler material like "Wagon Wheel." It is a song which, like many a Warhol silk-screen, feels emotionlessly churned out in order to reinforce the artist's brand. Warhol self-consciously embraced twentieth-century art's shift away from individual artworks as central focus, and toward the artist as celebrity. Warhol would rather Reed focus on building his catalog and public identity than on the meaningfulness of any one composition. The point of Andy Warhol is the recognizability of his name and the consistency of his persona and style. He pushed Reed to see himself the same way: he was one of the "Warhol Superstars," Andy's branded collection of bohemians whose artistic purpose was not located in their individual works, but in the fact that they were celebrities who produced art in association with Warhol.

Lou Reed's struggle with this self-conception—he felt both inspired by and resentful of Andy's patriarchal mentorship—feeds into *Transformer* as a whole and "Wagon Wheel" specifically. Though far from the best song on the album, it may in fact be one of the keys to what the album is about (or its purposeful lack of "about-ness" at all), and to the way Reed saw himself at this point in his career. One can imagine him, post-Velvet Underground, working as a typist for his father's accounting firm, having turned his back on a spotlight that never quite squarely landed on him, thinking how much he had failed to live up to Andy's vision of what he could have been. Had Lou-Reed-as-celebrity really failed so miserably? Or was he just being lazy?

Before long, the guilt catches up with him and he returns to churning out new songs. He's not yet a celebrity, but he will be if he can only churn out work that makes him seem like one. That's the kind of work he's got to produce if he's going to be a successful artist: work that buys into the myth of Lou Reed the Superstar. You've got to live your life as though you're number one.

Andy Warhol's influence, then, is another driving force behind Lou Reed's will to self-erasure. Besides self-hatred, besides a need to build his personality as a reaction to a hostile society, Lou's practice of making others believe that he is a blank slate was motivated by imitation of Andy. Both artists offer a vision of themselves as without personality, empty of content, detached and bored. "If you want to know all about Andy Warhol, just look at the surface of my paintings and films and me, and there I am," Warhol said in 1967. "There's nothing behind it."[2] Or in 1966, in a documentary film called *Artists: USA*, Warhol requests of an interviewer, "Why don't you just tell me the words and they'll just come out of my mouth?" He then proceeds to repeat the questions asked to him, minimally rephrased into first-person statements. Lou Reed can be seen in Australian TV footage from 1975 stealing the idea: "Why don't you just give me the answer and I'll repeat it?" Phrased another way, remember his claim: "I don't have a personality of my own."

The perverse fact that Lou inherited this view of himself from Andy makes it both more and less believable. His commitment to emptiness is so extreme that even his lack of a personal identity is copied from someone else. But it also reveals that quirk as itself inorganic, an intentional construction. Mirroring this self-defeating circle, a song like "Wagon Wheel" parrots conventions of contemporary rock music, containing nothing original. That's the point. This is not the expression of a person, Lou Reed wants us to believe, but the brand of an icon, a hollow form with no content.

---

[2]From a 1967 interview, quoted in Kynaston McShine, *Andy Warhol: A Retrospective*, exh. cat. (New York: Museum of Modern Art, 1989), 457.

"New York Telephone Conversation"
Lou and New York

"Oh my, and what shall we wear? / Oh my, and who really cares?" sings Reed on "New York Telephone Conversation." We've come to the most sarcastic song on *Transformer*. Which is kind of like saying the most German part of Germany, or the darkest part of a black hole. But the topics of this song—New York City and the hipster art and music scene therein—openly invite a seriously cynical take-down, and Reed rises to the occasion with a well-practised bitchiness that is sharper than ever.

New York City in the seventies was a hellhole; that is, violent crime was common, residents were poor, and standards of living were low. The intensity of living there led to the existence of various scenes that became of interest to the wider American public, such that New York in the seventies was particularly important for the history of music. Punk, disco, hip-hop, and house music all appeared as commercially viable genres when the music industry realized, more and more toward the end of that decade, the compellingness of the myriad cultures sprouting up like new breeds of mushroom from the unchecked pile of shit that was the City. Unsupervised young criminals with nothing better to do, it turns out, are sometimes quite interesting people.

At the same time, New York was a high culture hub and tourist destination. Broadway shows, art museums, and historic landmarks all testified to NYC as a great place for people with money to hang out—rampant heroin problem, failing infrastructure, and high rates of white flight to the suburbs notwithstanding. It's a recipe for a mugging, or a more high-profile mass-swindle such as groups like Blondie and the Ramones pulled off. The poor kids are going to take the rich people's money, be it via assault or selling records.

Anyone suddenly interested in Lou Reed in 1972 or 73 is neatly analogous to a clueless tourist in New York in the seventies. They think it's Broadway; they think it's the Statue of Liberty. It's actually addiction, poverty, and criminalized sex. How cute all these touristic bisexuals or people popping reds for the first time must have been to Lou. He's a speed freak who's been ass-fucked by a stranger on a decaying abandoned pier at 3:00 a.m. You can understand why he might be skeptical of a scene fixated on trendy faux-sleaze, or a little sarcastic as he becomes its poster-boy. "Who has touched and who has dabbled, here in the city of shows?" he snaps.

All of which is why Lou Reed writing songs for a Broadway musical, as Andy Warhol proposed in 1970 or 71, is kind of an amazing idea. Think of it! Lou Reed as Stephen Sondheim. It almost happened. Fresh off the successful first run of *Pork*, Warhol was emboldened to envision such a spectacle. He asked Reed to write the songs, and Reed pulls it off, which is only surprising if you're thinking of him as the guy who wrote "Waiting for the Man" rather than "After Hours." He's versatile; he's better than he lets on. He can write you any type of song you want, if he could only work up the motivation. And no one gets him motivated like his judgmental, productivity-obsessed father figure Andy.

Here he applies the concept of "The Telephone Hour" from *Bye Bye Birdie* to the world of adult hipsters in lower Manhattan, and sharpens it into a minute and a half of white-hot disdain. This is the phenomenon of Lou Reed incongruously placed into a more audience-friendly format—which, if *Transformer* were a concept album, would be the concept—at its most acute. If, as in "Satellite of Love," what happens when you ask him to write a hit single is apathy and hostility filtered through soaring melody, so too with a comic-relief Broadway number: it's the same pissed-off boredom, but with jazz hands. Lester Bangs in a 1973 article aptly compared the alcoholic, declining Reed to "a deaf-mute in a telephone booth" (admitting, however, that Reed himself had come up with the phrase). Lou Reed, in front of the biggest audience of his life, is utterly out of place, holding a receiver that he has no hope of using. The whole album is him with superstardom in the palm of his hand, saying, "Oh, great. *Just* what I needed."

Sarcasm is an effort to assert power, which also reveals it as a confession of vulnerability. So this is Lou's battle with a New York scene—or even a broader Western pop culture, which to a New Yorker is the same thing—that threatens to define, pigeonhole, and dominate him. He disdains it because he's afraid of it. Note that the song begins with "stop calling me" and ends with "please, pick up!" If you're a fan of Lou

Reed, whether a record buyer or a friend of his, he hates you but he needs you. He hates you *because* he needs you.

This dynamic is an inherent property of being a serious performer of any kind, varying only in its intensity. If your livelihood and self-respect depend on hordes of people paying attention to you, you will end up with some amount of resentment of those hordes and the terrifying sway their whims hold over you. If they like you, you're rich; if they hate you, you're a failure. Some people feel the same way about people they love. We depend on the people we love, which is why we get so upset when they don't love us back. Notice this and you've found the Rosetta Stone of anger; it's all various translations of insecurity.

A sarcastic love song, as this one might be called, is love thinly disguised as anger thinly disguised as love again. Like *Transformer* as a whole, it's an impersonation of an impersonation of itself. What, indeed, is going on at the end of this song when Reed sings, "For I know this night will kill me if I can't be with you / If I can't be with you," straining his voice at the end for the cliché showtune big finish? Is he joking or is he serious? Is he in character, or singing as himself? Nine songs into the record, is there even a difference anymore?

"I'm So Free"
Lou and Freedom

Lou Reed is known for being hostile to the press. He walks out of interviews, insults people to their face, answers monosyllabically, and generally acts like a jerk. There are a few interviews I've seen, however, where this set of attitudes transcends hostility and becomes something like an art form of its own.

My favorite is a 1974 meeting with various pop culture journalists in Sydney, Australia, edited footage of which was broadcast on Australian public television. The interviewers are baiting him with questions about drugs and sex, trying to get him to be outrageous. He remains more than calm; he seems heavily sedated (it's possible, even probable that he was). His composure and commitment are amazing. As someone who's sat through uncountable bad interviews, I am intimately familiar with how hard it is not to submit, in your answer, to the interviewers' tone and thus their worldview. Lou doesn't give an inch. He knows that the game being played is to try to gain control of the story, and to subtly degrade him. The press wants him to look out-of-control, because that's what fascinates people about him: his decadence, his being unmoored from morality or reality. And they are trying to see how much they can get him to inhabit the cartoonish, "sleazy" persona they have imagined is his. In this conversation, they lose and he wins. He stays utterly true to his own tone, and tells them nothing.

> Q: Do you think it's a decadent society we're living in?
> LOU REED: No.
> Q: Would you describe yourself as a decadent person?
> LR: No.
> Q: How would you describe yourself?
> LR: Average.
> Q: It said in your release that we were given this morning that you like lying to the press, why is this, now you're doing it now.
> LR: I didn't say that, the release did.
> Q: Is it true?
> LR: No.[1]

With every parry and thrust, they open a trap which he proceeds to cleanly sidestep. Later, in my favorite moment of the interview, the gloves come off and the questioners admit what they're really asking him:

> Q: Lou, you sing a lot about transvestites and sadomasochism. Uh, how would you describe yourself in the light of these songs?
> LR: I . . . What does that have to do with me?
> Q: Well, could I put it bluntly, and pardon the question: are you a transvestite or a homosexual?

[1] "Lou Reed meets the Australian press in 1974." YouTube video, 5:25. Posted by "ABC News (Australia)," uploaded October 27, 2013. https://www.youtube.com/watch?v=RbE2zNoWPFw.

LR: Sometimes.

Q: Which one?

LR: I don't know. What's the difference?

Q: Why do you like being—why do you like describing yourself as this? Why do you think you fit into this type of person?

LR: It's something to do.

Q: Is life so boring to you, then?

LR: No.

Q: What do you like most in life?

LR: Everything.

Q: Are there any things you like better than others?

LR: No.[2]

In this exchange is one of the most direct examples of Lou Reed the queer at war with the straight world, the unexamined hostility from the heterosexual questioner engendering in Reed a blank nihilism that masks pure fury. Pushed to explain or justify his sexuality and gender, he denies the very terms of the conversation. His road to freedom from the oppressive setup—you're an aberration and there's something wrong with you, explain yourself—is through the assertion of all-encompassing meaninglessness.

Here's my decoded rewrite of the chess match going on in this conversation:

Q: Why are you a degenerate faggot?

LR: Well, it's just a way of being a person, like any other.

[2]Ibid.

Q: Is life so boring to you, then? Are you a degenerate
   because you hate everybody and hate life and are
   generally morally corrupt?
LR: No, I love life.
Q: Explain how.
LR: No.

If you've been reading this book wondering why someone
who has so many negative things to say about Lou Reed
would choose to write a book about Lou Reed and call him
a hero, this is why. This crystallizes the way in which Reed's
nihilistic orientation is, in fact, a successful retaliation to a
culture that treats him like dirt. Whatever you say he is, that's
what he's not, because he's learned that to let anyone else
define him is to let himself be demeaned. He's not anything
for which you have prepared, in advance, a reductive name
and meaning. He is a transformer.

* * *

Still, though, Lou Reed, the Rock 'n' Roll Animal, is a caged
creature, and "I'm So Free" is the proof. He repeats the title
phrase over thirty times in this song. The lady doth protest
too much, methinks.

Or maybe I've got the terms of the conversation wrong.
Maybe for Lou, freedom's not such a great time. Maybe it's
just another word for nothing left to lose. If to be free is to
be a pill-popping alcoholic in a doomed, abusive marriage,
show me into the cage, please.

I can see the ways in which Lou Reed is correct in calling
himself free. "I do what I want," he sings, and that does seem

true. He's his own boss, and he's fought for that. But a freedom from all constraints is its own kind of prison. He goes on to sing ". . . and I want what I see," suggesting that to do what he wants is to be enslaved to his own whim, the tyranny of desire. To be as radically unconstrained as *Transformer*-era Lou Reed is to move so far from puritanism into hedonism that you end up as you started: paralyzed. Whatever he sees, he does, bound by instinct like a dog that can't stop itself from humping a stranger's leg.

This singer's vision of freedom involves seeing every identity as a jail and every person as a cop. He's not just free, he's "so free." He's more than free because he's obsessed with freedom, and he's obsessed with freedom because he sees threats to his freedom at every turn. Marriage is a threat. Sobriety is a threat. Failure is a threat. Success is a threat. Anything that involves commitment is a threat. The various arenas in which he has a sense of himself as a persecuted outlaw—as a queer, as a bohemian, as a struggling artist, as a drug user—have compounded into a desperate inner drama in which everyone is out to shackle him, and he can only rely on his own ontological slipperiness to avoid imprisonment.

Lou Reed finds freedom via constant transformation, which amounts to a kind of constant failure. If you don't commit, you don't get hurt; you never have to fully be anything, and you never *get to* fully be anything. Reed's ambitions are negative; they are to not be what he despises rather than to be anything he affirms. "I'm gonna try to nullify my life," he wrote at age twenty-two, as a formerly suburban kid becoming a great artist and disavowing his personal history. He would disavow *Transformer* as well: "I like all the old Velvets records;

I don't like Lou Reed records," he told Lester Bangs in 1976.[3] A painful past gives rise to a compulsion to move on, to shed anything and everything and become someone no one else can figure out. Freedom, indeed, would be to have nothing left to lose. Oh, sweet nuthin'.

"I'm So Free" is both less and more nihilistic than earlier songs in which Reed declares/longs for his freedom. Less, because it's an enthusiastic assertion of ego; more, because it asserts ego to the point of losing all empathy for anyone else. "Yes I am Mother Nature's Son," he tells us, "and I'm the only one." He is the center of the universe, better than the Beatles[4] and heir to the Earth itself. Nevertheless—or by the same token—he is barely there, barely human.

Something has clearly shifted in the three years since the Velvet Underground recorded this song's predecessor, "I'm Set Free." That song is hymnlike, a kind of rewrite of "Amazing Grace" which finds Reed in a moment of sudden clarity of vision, yet knowing that his freedom will only lead

---

[3]"How To Succeed in Torture Without Really Trying," originally published in April 1976 issue of *Creem*, compiled in *Psychotic Reactions and Carburetor Dung*, ed. Greil Marcus. "I like *Berlin* and I positively LOVE *Metal Machine Music*," he goes on, once again betraying that there is a real person in his music between the waves of nihilist commercialism and laziness, daring the discerning true believers to search out the real thing.

[4]Do I detect another cocky Beatles ripoff in the lyric "could only happen to me," cf. "I Should Have Known Better?" Lou is trying to wrest the rock 'n' roll crown from the Beatles, recently dethroned by their break-up. Not you, he tells them twice, but me. I'm Mother Nature's *only* son, this could only happen to *me*. I realize I may be reading these lyrics a little too closely at this point. God help me, I can't stop.

him to "find a new illusion." This is Zen Lou. All is illusory, including the Self that is fooled by these illusions. This is a peaceful version of what much of the Velvet Underground's music was about: finding freedom by way of self-destruction. Which is to say, destruction of the Self, of the Ego. Have you noticed how many Velvet Underground songs involve someone's head being cut open, cut off, blown apart, or split in two? Listen again: *White Light/White Heat* was a covert concept album. Every song (except the taciturn "Here She Comes Now") mentions a destroyed cranium, and a tattoo of an impaled skull is barely visible on the black-on-black cover. "I'm Set Free," on the following album, continued this beheading theme, exulting, "I saw my head laughing, rolling on the ground, and now I'm set free." There, it rings true. He sounds like he's made a spiritual breakthrough—which may be fleeting, but everything is.

If the Velvet Underground mentioned self-destruction but were really talking about freedom, "I'm So Free" mentions freedom but is really about self-destruction—freedom's funhouse mirror image, its cruel parody. It's an understandable thing to write about, considering Lou's transition from a frustrated artist longing for commercial success to a successful sell-out trapped in its jaws. To succeed commercially is to finally make it to the other side of the steel bars that have caged you, only to find that you're in the other half of a closed cell, and that the bars divide it neatly in two. "I'm So Free" is a song by a man trapped in a prison made of hollow clichés, in thrall to the false idol of rock 'n' roll freedom. Rock star Lou Reed, on tour doing "whatever he wants," does not have freedom, but *license*: license to do drugs, to have casual sex, to stay up late, to sneer at authority. As Bruce Springsteen put it, "Personal license [is] to freedom as masturbation [is] to sex. It's not bad, but it's not the real deal."[5]

Yes, Lou Reed has found his new illusion, and it is a dream of personal rock 'n' roll license that even he, blind drunk and high on amphetamines, knows is not the real deal. The lyric begins with bragging so over-the-top ("I'm the only one / I do what I want") that he can't possibly mean it, or at least not after the speed wears off. The song, even as it claims total self-sufficiency, begs to be heard as a cry for help. This is one of many moments on *Transformer* that is so much about subtext that there's almost no text; in fact, it's the very blandness of the text that points you toward the subtext.

Reed's unconscious occasionally tries to surface here and is quickly pushed back down by the insistent choruses. The second verse is a plea to St. Germain, a legendary figure in the theosophical teaching of occultist Alice Bailey, who Reed had been reading about and referencing in songs and interviews since at least 1967 (the song "White Light/White Heat" obliquely referred to Bailey's *Treatise on White Magic*, as did certain subsequent VU songs). Reed's oft-overlooked interest in Theosophy and the New Age movement was his principal spiritual outlet in the late sixties and early seventies, and his recurring off-hand invocations of it read like secret messages to those in the know. When it comes up in "I'm So Free," a song about self-mastery and independence, it stands out as an admission of weakness.

[5]Bruce Springsteen, *Born to Run* (New York: Simon and Schuster, 2014). https://lareviewofbooks.org/article/trouble-in-the-heartland/#!.

But it's the title phrase, repeated ad nauseam in a voice that fails to match the energy of the spirited music, that creates the real dramatic irony. Declaring his freedom again and again, Reed demonstrates his powerlessness. Any effectiveness of the track—one of the record's weakest—comes from the tension produced by this disconnect. Those moments when a person begins to realize just how unfree they are, when they realize how titanic the struggle against their restraints will be, can produce some truly compelling pop music. Lou Reed's not there yet, but he will be soon. Springsteen became a great artist not when he pulled his car out of his "town full of losers," exulting in his youthful freedom, but when he realized that he could not escape the ties that bind, and that real freedom lay within. One can feel Lou Reed approaching this realization like the lip of a dark canyon, and the drama of the moment fascinates.

"Goodnight Ladies"
Lou and Loneliness

At the end of the night, when most of the partygoers have left and the rest have passed out drunk, you and Lou Reed are the only people left standing. Or maybe collapsed on a couch together, wasted but still hanging onto consciousness. All night he's been alternating between glowering silently near the bar and talking everyone's ear off about everything—whether ranting about whoever's pissing him off lately or telling sly jokes in questionable taste—always with a rapidly vanishing vodka martini in hand, always threatening to leave, never taking off his macho black leather jacket. It's been hard to tell what his deal is. One minute he's spouting off gay rights slogans and the next he's talking shit about some pathetic effeminate faggot acquaintance. At some point in the evening someone who knows him a bit better reassured you, *Oh, don't mind Lou. He doesn't mean a word of it.*

Now, at 4:00 a.m., heads lolling back on a couch bedecked in spilled drinks and stray glitter, things start to get weird. Lou starts confessing things, suddenly with an air of credibility that's been missing from everything else he's said. He knows you're the only one listening, you probably won't remember any of this, and who would believe you if you told them anyway?

Hang on, he says after this has gone on a while. There's something I want to show you.

When he returns he's wearing a corset, a frilly black fascinator, feathers, thigh-high stockings with straps and buckles, the whole bit. You're drunk enough to wonder if this is really happening. He puts the needle to an old record, the tuba and drums start up, and, with a kick of a high heel, Lou Reed sings: "Goodnight, ladies—ladies, goodnight."

*   *   *

Closing tracks come with a sense of weightiness and finality. We expect a kind of resolution from our endings, that anything left unsaid will now be said. So at the end of an album stuffed with misdirection, half-truths, and red herrings, we want "Goodnight Ladies" to be the moment when all masks have fallen away. This final statement, a listener's appetite tells her, will be a sincere one, and now we will see at last who Lou Reed really is. Though the album is often unsatisfying, here it does not disappoint: "Goodnight Ladies" is the perfect resolution, and it comes, surprisingly but inevitably, in the form of a burlesque pastiche, the picture of a show-stopping finale in the vaudeville tradition.

When one thinks of unvarnished artistic realness, one probably does not think of the vaudeville era. At least, one who's a big Lou Reed fan probably doesn't. Fans of seventies rock music are more likely to associate raw truth-telling with the brash social realism of The Clash, the visceral minimalism of Suicide, or the primitive intensity of Iggy Pop. Certainly it is those musicians who, as the seventies wore on, seemed to take up the principal artistic concerns of Lou Reed, creating punk rock as they did so. Punk is celebrated for its back-to-basics simplicity, aggression, and independence of the concern for commercial appeal, not to mention the sheer freshness of its sounds. Being a major inspiration for that raw, realist musical movement is at the top of Reed's list of accomplishments. Why, then, do I claim that this old-timey showbiz number reveals the "real" Lou Reed?

I guess what I'm trying to point out is that *Transformer* ends with the triumph of a suppressed femininity.

You'll notice that my go-to examples of the punks most likely to be seen as "real" are all male. Punk's association of masculinity with authenticity is not unique among subgenres of rock music. Rock is a classic example of a boys' club. The women present in the genre have to fight discouragement both passive and active, and their legitimacy as part of the respected canon is continually overlooked or questioned. Misogyny and sexism are present in literally every corner of Western culture, and punk—generally socially progressive agenda notwithstanding—is far from immune. Homophobia and transphobia, even more so, were taken for granted as normal attitudes among heterosexuals in the early seventies, and were only beginning to be seen as reprehensible prejudices in socially liberal circles.

So while any woman in rock music was met with waves of unmistakable skepticism and belittlement, a man or male-bodied person who performed femininity faced open derision and disgust. Both were likely to deal with the threat of violence, sexual or otherwise. Any femininity entering the male space of rock provokes misogyny of varying intensities and types. Even the hip straight folks, the ones who claimed to be down with whatever adventurous sex people were into, were palpably disdainful of the effeminate male—see for unsubtle example Nick Tosches's backhanded contemporary review of *Transformer* in *Rolling Stone* magazine, in which he advises Reed to "forget this artsyfartsy kind of homo stuff and just go in there with a bad hangover and start blaring out his visions of lunar assfuck."

Not surprising, then, that the album hides its femininity at first, opening with the macho kiss-off of "Vicious," in which Reed threatens violence before anyone can threaten him. "Vicious" is the psychotic outburst your first week in jail so everyone knows not to fuck with you. The record's first half doesn't quite commit to any personal gender subversion, merely gesturing obliquely toward it (Andy's Chest) or detachedly describing it in others (Walk on the Wild Side). But the second side immediately and increasingly reveals Lou Reed's interest in camp, flamboyance and femininity, starting with "Make Up" and culminating in "Goodnight Ladies." Like the side-by-side photos on the album's back cover of a visibly erect motorcycle tough and a stage-ready starlet, our singer has transformed from James Dean to Marilyn Monroe. The veil of masculinity has fallen away completely, revealing the femme buried under the butch.

Not to overlook the fact that this entire song is heavily armored in irony and potential claims of sarcasm or parody. You might hear Reed as sounding droll and sarcastic here— that option is open to us as listeners almost everywhere on *Transformer*. The genre-aping of "Goodnight Ladies" is a perfect cover-up, really. There is an inauthenticity baked into vaudeville and burlesque, a guiding ethic of stagey tricks being played on the audience, and therefore a disdain for honesty. Which is essentially the same reason straight men get away with dressing in drag or acting effeminate in theater productions and not having their manhood questioned: it's a *show*, it's a *gag*. They don't really mean it. But when Lou Reed does gay musical theater send-up three times in the course of six songs, one starts to doubt his supposed insincerity. By the time he caps off his pop debut with a draggy Broadway finale, he's no longer making fun of campy faggotry, he's fully inhabiting it.

This is the furthest Lou seems to have gone into this mode of performance, and he didn't often return to it later in his career. The tough-guy leather jacket and sunglasses are the far more dominant self-presentation he uses, before and after *Transformer* and concurrent public appearances. His glam/femme approach is very clearly the exception to his normal behavior. What gave him the space—creative, social, and psychological—to behave this flamingly?

For that I believe we can thank the legendary David Bowie. "The whole glam thing was kind of great for me, when I met Bowie and he was into that, and so I got into that," said Lou. "But all it was, was it was something I had already seen with Warhol. But I hadn't done that. So the seventies was like, a chance for me to get in on it, and since no one knew me from Adam particularly, I could say I was anything, be any way."[1] Reed had permission, via his relative anonymity as well as

---

[1] *Lou Reed Remembered*, 32:20. Directed by Chris Rodley. United Kingdom: BBC 4, 2013.

Bowie's suddenly trendy sequins and dresses, to at last look as fabulous as all his old Factory trans femme friends.

David Bowie, more than legitimating transgenderism as part of rock music's concept of sincerity in performance, simply removed the sincerity. This allowed men to display femininity without having their masculinity called into serious question. By making it clear that he wasn't ever quite showing his cards or confessing deep personal truths in his music—he cast himself as an alien from another planet—he could cherry-pick from the world of fashion across gender lines, across any and all taboos. Because he didn't mean it. He was acting. And yet, like a seemingly tongue-in-cheek Halloween costume, this kind of "all in good fun" rule-bending allowed authentically transgender people a foot in the door, a precedent for showing up in pop culture performing gender on their own terms.

Lou Reed—as usual—lay somewhere in between. He was never a trans woman or committed to drag, but his breaking from gender roles came from a sincere queerness more than Bowie's no-rules stagecraft did. Reed consistently queered pop culture's vision of masculinity, often without even trying to, just by having an instinctive tendency to androgyny. On "Goodnight Ladies," though, we see him do it on purpose, going all-out burlesque. Tongue in cheek or not, the macho bullshit dissipates, and the lace stockings win out as the listener's final image of what a pop star might be.

*　*　*

But the darker, more subtle coming out that can be heard on "Goodnight Ladies" is not gendered, but emotional.

Lou waits until the closing track to admit the plain fact undergirding the whole rest of the record: that he's lonely. The only other openly sad song, "Perfect Day," never quite states its sadness straight out, but lets the exceptional peace of the fleeting moment combine with mournful music to imply a malaise-filled life surrounding that moment. Here, inversely, playful backing music tries and, if you're listening, fails to obscure direct confessions of emotional desperation. "I'm still missing my other half," Lou sings, half-hoping we still think he's being sarcastic. "It must be something I did in the past / Don't it just make you want to laugh? It's a lonely Saturday night." Sounds cute when you first hear it. But consider that this is a gay man, engaged to a woman, singing about a permanent sense of incompleteness. He blames himself and then can't help but chuckle, alone in his apartment instead of out with friends.

This, at last, is real pain stated directly. But it takes a campy musical artifice complete with sarcastic tuba and clarinet for him to be able to say it.[2] As the lyrics reveal more, the woozy brass and woodwind section plays more busily, upping the theatricality. Lou vocally matches this increasing musical silliness, dropping more vibrato into the long notes, mocking the cartoonish drama of a Broadway star at the

---

[2] These lines—starting with "I'm still missing my other half"—are heard immediately at the opening of the song in its earliest recorded version, a home demo played on acoustic guitar in which the phrase "Goodnight Ladies" does not yet appear. It seems likely that these were the first words he wrote for the song. For the album, he buries them deep in the track, after two and a half minutes of ironic stylistic padding to throw the listener off the trail.

big moments: "And at eleven o'clock I watch the network neewwwsss." Once it's clear that the whole thing is a send-up, he can drop lines like "Something tells me that you're really gone" without worrying that anyone might think he really means it or feels anything.

This is not his first foray into painful confession playfully sung. 1969's *The Velvet Underground*, which I'm beginning to think of as a sister album to this one, ends on a highly similar note: "After Hours," sung by Velvets drummer Mo Tucker. In both songs, an old-fashioned melody pairs with a lyric envying all the people having fun and being in love to suggest a bottomless chasm of despair. But while Tucker's delivery sidesteps sappiness by sounding almost disturbingly naïve, Reed (now bereft of bandmates to whom he can cede the too-revealing spotlight) avoids the purely maudlin via an all-consuming boredom. Lou Reed at age thirty has retreated even further into irony, because he's in more personal turmoil. A few years back he could sing "Pale Blue Eyes" with an unambiguous sincerity we almost never hear from him in the seventies. Post-Velvet Underground, he's less integrated, has more to hide, and thus is wearing a more opaque veil: the veil of *Who on Earth could take this shit seriously?*

Well, plainly, Lou Reed could. The title and refrain of "Goodnight Ladies" quotes the mad Ophelia in Shakespeare's *Hamlet* and, more directly, the second section of T. S. Eliot's "The Waste Land."[3] Though it's possible that this is a snobby

---

[3]This is not Reed's first lyrical shout-out to T. S. Eliot. For instance, "Between thought and expression / lies a lifetime," on "Some Kinda Love," was a paraphrase of Eliot's "The Hollow Men."

collegiate reference for its own sake without much content, the song resonates fascinatingly with the poem's extended scene, set in a bar at closing time, of a woman advising the wife of a returning soldier to "make yourself a bit smart" because "he wants a good time / And if you don't give it him, there's others will." The theme of feminine inadequacy ramps up as the bartender announces "HURRY UP PLEASE IT'S TIME" with increasing frequency, and the narrator's comments become more biting: "You ought to be ashamed, I said, to look so antique. / (And her only thirty-one.)" Reed's song draws on the same anxieties about beauty that fades with age, no longer sufficient to please its intended audience, as he closes a record that he fears has arrived too late to lead to lasting success.

To reference T. S. Eliot and Shakespeare in a pop song is pretentious. I don't mean that as an insult. It's pretentious in the best way, that is, it suggests artistic ambition, and that he indeed takes this shit seriously. Lou Reed wants to be in league with Eliot and Shakespeare as a writer, and this ambition pushes him to write better songs, to rise above the rote rock songwriting of "Wagon Wheel" and "I'm So Free." But he cloaks these ambitions in irony, an escape hatch if anyone accuses him of pretension. Reed means for his songs to function as literature, but he also needs them to function as disposable and insincere Pop. Nevertheless, the sincerity shows through.

A song is a bad place to hide. Songs are always built to reveal their authors' inner lives—it's inherent to the form. You can dress your song up in jokey costumes, bury it in noise, or fill it with lies, but if you dare to sing it, you will reveal things about yourself. Having spent years trying it a million different ways, I've learned this beyond a doubt. Singing is confession.

In "Goodnight Ladies," dressed up in anachronistic frills and lace, Lou confesses one of the true thesis statements of *Transformer*: that he wishes he could be a star, but he knows he can't. This whole enterprise was doomed from the start, a pathetic joke, an utter failure. At 3:15, where we might expect the song to start wrapping up or fading out, the band breaks from its drunken swoon into emphatic staccato, underlining the lyrical phrases as a Broadway orchestra might do to hammer home a crucial plot point: "If I was an actor, or a dancer who is glamorous / Then you know an amorous life would soon be mine." The conclusion he reaches at the end of *Transformer*, his career reinvention as a glam rock star, is that he's not glamorous and that he can't act. However much he might like to be at times, he's not David Bowie and he can't pretend to be. He can only be his unglamorous self, staying at home drinking alone, watching the news at eleven.

Ending the record with this song is Reed's defiant rebuttal to the idea—held closely by his fans, David Bowie, and even himself—that it is his destiny to achieve rock stardom. This song's attitude is in direct contrast to Bowie's grand vision of celebrity artifice. David Bowie made himself into an extraterrestrial messiah, a strange creature the world has never seen before—or at the very least, an actor who is glamorous. Lou Reed reminds us again and again in his songs that he is utterly average and boring. Part of what made Bowie great is his ambitious aim to take us on a strange odyssey through a fantastic dystopia. Reed's appeal, on the other hand, is his matter-of-fact realism about the dystopia we're already living in, where everybody's anesthetized, watching TV. He is a common lonely drunk, and if you thought he was going to transform into a glam superstar alien like Bowie, you were sorely mistaken.

It doesn't mean it doesn't hurt, though. Again, as in "Satellite of Love," he's been left behind, with a bottle of gin and a color television for numbing comfort, pretending not to be jealous. We are left with the sense that a deeper transformation is, in fact, not an option. Despite the costume changes he has undergone from "Vicious" to "Goodnight Ladies," he's still the same loser. He can put on the burlesque outfit, but it's not going to fit. He's just not star material. Like in "Make Up," he does long for change—"it'd be so nice to fall in love" —but he's destined to fail: "people say that it's impossible."

So *Transformer* seems to end in stasis, a failure to have transformed at all. The whole thing has been a bitter joke. Lou Reed, a pop star? Yeah, right, he says. Nothing could be more ridiculous. Why, I might as well put on this tiara and these lacy tights. See? Absurd. And why not throw in a sequined bodice and thick eyeliner, while we're being absurd. Rouge, lipstick, glitter? Sure, pile 'em on. See, see what a grotesque laugh it all is?

All right, I'm ready for my close-up.

The Man Himself

You can't meet a legend in person. Because legends aren't people; legends are myths, and myths aren't real. Which is why I'm not totally sure what happened when I met Lou Reed. He was my hero, I performed two of his songs while he watched, and I talked to him for less time than it takes to listen to "New York Telephone Conversation." At age twenty-one, I experienced the meeting as one of the most thrilling honors I could imagine. Because of his name, because of his old records. Not because of who he actually was at that moment, or what we said to each other that day, March 13, 2008. I was so buzzed on his legend that I could barely hear or see him. I did not make real contact with him. He may have met me, but I didn't meet him.

That afternoon I'm nervously waiting around backstage pre-show, having done a quick soundcheck with my band. There's a lot of waiting around in the life of a professional musician. I notice a guy with a shaved head and black-framed glasses pacing back and forth, wringing his hands. After he passes me a few times, I realize it's Moby, the well-known (legendary!) DJ and electronica musician. "God damn," he says out loud to himself, stopping near me.

It seems like he's fishing for a response. I'm the only one around. "What's up?" I ask, fighting not to be starstruck—this being the guy who made *Play*, an album I and most people my age I knew loved throughout the eighth grade.

> "Oh, nothing," he says distractedly. "I just don't really know what I'm doing here. I'm supposed to perform with Lou Reed tonight."
>
> "Wow. Yeah, that's a big deal."
>
> "I don't know why he wants me to do it. We make different kinds of music; it's not really a good fit. I don't get why he likes me. But he asked me to do a duet with him."
>
> "Holy shit. What are you singing?"
>
> "'Walk On the Wild Side.' I'm so fucking nervous. It just doesn't make sense. He's, like, a legend."

I have to admit, it's a weird pairing. But then, I don't know how I've ended up on the bill either. I tend to think choosing an unexpected partner to perform with is a characteristic Lou Reed move. "Don't worry. You'll do great," I tell him. He's making me even more nervous than I already am. Moby's a seasoned professional, a star in his own right; I'm the amateur here. "Good luck," I tell him lamely.

"Thanks. You too." He paces away from me. I walk off to go find my band. The guitarist and drummer are milling around near some Port-a-Potties. "Where's Job?" I ask. Job is the bassist.

"I think he's throwing up. He's really nervous." I relate; I'm jittery as hell. This is going to be the largest crowd we've ever played for, our first time at the South-by-Southwest festival, and fucking Lou Reed is supposedly going to be there. We've only been together as a band for two years, playing small college venues and nearly empty dive bars. This is a huge leap upward for us in every way.

We're on after Yo La Tengo, who do charmingly gentle versions of "I Found A Reason" and "She's My Best Friend." I take the stage with an acoustic guitar to play "Heroin," all on my own in front of a packed courtyard of rowdy drunks. And of course the fucking guitar isn't making any sound. The cable's busted or something. Story of my life. My bandmates frantically run onstage and help me troubleshoot.

We get it together before too long and I start playing and improvising a monologue about my disgust with the ubiquity of corporate sponsorship at the festival. I play a hyper, nervous "Heroin" that has none of the sedated visionary quality of the original and all of the anxiety of my square, suburban, drug-free youth. It seems to connect anyhow— there is a headlong reaching out for death in the song that I am able to commune with. The crowd cheers and shouts some of the lyrics. The adrenaline I feel is insane. I'm not on amphetamines, but I may as well be.

The band joins me onstage for "New Age," a favorite of mine which always struck me as underrated. Nothing goes wrong. That was the goal. But it's during this song that I notice, standing in the front row, Lou Reed, sixty-six years old but looking eighty, fancy Leica camera on a strap around his neck. He snaps a photograph. My brain feels like it's on fire. What has happened in my life that this is possible?

We finish up. They rush us offstage; Mark Kozelek is on next. Lou's right there, stage-side, wearing an unremarkable t-shirt and slacks. I am bathing in visions of the Velvet Underground. The tongue of rock 'n' roll history is slowly licking my face.

Lou holds out his hand and we touch. We shake hands. This is actually happening; this is real; I can feel his fingers. This man is literally the reason I became a professional musician. More than that: my life was saved by rock 'n' roll. *His* rock 'n' roll. The Velvet Underground opened a door in my teenage head that was an escape hatch from a suffocating self that didn't work for me anymore. From his voice and music, I intuited a way of being human, of being real, of being free, that allowed me to survive.

I must have hesitated. He speaks first. "That was a great version of 'Heroin,'" he says.

What the hell am I supposed to say? I forget to thank him. "Aw, I bet you say that to all the bands."

"Don't bet on it," he grunts. Bluntly cutting through bullshit, always.

I'm tongue tied.

"Are you doing heroin?" he asks.

I'm not sure what the right answer is. I go with the truth: "No."

"Good."

And that's it. He heads backstage; I gather my guitar and cables, my psyche melting into a warm liquid goo. This little music career, so early on, has reached its peak and entirely justified itself.

* * *

Of course, as you the reader know by now, I can't help but overanalyze these things. Why didn't I talk to him more? Why didn't I say something clever, something true? All I did was doubt his sincerity—*I bet you say that to all the bands* plays over in over in my head while I curse myself—to which he responded by insisting (albeit with a sarcastic edge, "don't bet on it") that he was sincere. In thirty seconds we enacted his audience's distrust of his authenticity and the charged backlash it provokes in him. Of course he's not bullshitting me. He's never had any time for the faintest glimmer of bullshit. Even when he outright lies, he's one of the realest motherfuckers in the game.

And then that question: "Are you doing heroin?" Again— it's like an illness; just as I have to write pages of analysis of what is essentially a simple rock record, so too am I bound to dig through the layers of a plainspoken four-word sentence—I wonder if he *really* meant the question, or if he knew the answer before he asked. Maybe I somehow looked to him like a heroin addict. Or maybe this was his tit-for-tat response to my skepticism of his compliment, him telling me, *I see right through you. You're a fake. You'd never touch a needle. You're a suburban middle-class Jew who's never once stepped out of bounds.*

He'd have been right; that's what I was, which is why he was the worshipped, and I the worshipper. He came from pretty much the exact same place I did, but he bravely broke free. Obviously, shooting heroin is an idiotic and hopeless thing to do, which he acknowledged ("Good."), but his willingness to try it was symptomatic of the spirit of adventure that made him great. For better or for worse, he took risks and utterly transformed his destiny. His life, and even this miniscule bit of conversation, was a challenge to me to do the same.

Or maybe we were just making small talk. When you're as enthralled by a Legend as I was—am—the small looms large. Eleven songs become a book. A rock record fundamentally alters the course of your life.

* * *

The hours go by, the sun goes down, the bands play everybody's favorites. Two songs per band. Moby's on last. I don't see Lou Reed anywhere. Maybe he got bored and left? I'm worried for Moby. He's got a blonde female singer with him; they do a decent "Femme Fatale"; she's weakly aping Nico's lead vocals. There's a weirdly long delay after the song wraps up. Moby leaves the microphone and is talking to someone at the side of the stage. Everyone's holding their breath. Rumor had it that Lou was closing out the evening. But it'd be so like him to just ditch it.

Moby returns to the mic and says, to our relief, "He's here." Lou walks out holding a guitar and everybody goes nuts. He's dead-eyed, stone-faced, as always. Dutifully plugs in the guitar. The other two guitar players get a drone going in the key of D and Reed starts the laid-back strumming pattern of "Wild Side." There's no drummer, no bassists to imitate the hooky dueling bass lines. Just three electric guitar players. It's a little stiff and mechanical. You have to wonder how long it's been since he's played this one. But he starts singing and you realize that he wrote this shit nearly four decades ago. He's not the Lou Reed most of us fell in love with; there's probably no shred of that person left in him by now. He's doing karaoke. This, too, is a cover band.

He doesn't say "Hey, babe." He just goes "She says," leaves the space and then sings, "Take a walk on the wild side." Moby takes the second verse, terrified. There's not much chemistry between the two singers; one doesn't get the sense that they're good friends. Then again, Lou Reed never looks like he's anybody's friend. He's a stone wall. I find out later that the two are in fact quite close, which only shows how hard Lou is to read. Nevertheless, the song seems under-rehearsed. A couple other women have joined the blonde "Femme Fatale" singer; the trio does a decent job with the "doot-da-doo" line, but then later Lou starts singing it unexpectedly, awkwardly forcing them to join in with him. He's conducting the band as he goes. I don't doubt that he's the one departing from the original arrangement, operating on instinct and ego.

By the end, a drummer arrives and joins in, the guitars have beefed up, the droning D-strings get louder, and we are under the spell of a classic Lou Reed sonic assault. I start to understand the power of his stiff mechanicalism, which struck me as embarrassing and lazy at first. His boredom offsets the exuberance of the kind of loud rock 'n' roll we've all become numb to, just as the guitars' one-note drone grounds the arrangement, allowing it to be as wild as it wants without ever losing track of the mood. It may be an emotional defense mechanism—I never cared about this song anyway, says the singer, so big deal if you don't like it, or me—but it's also an extremely effective *musical* defense mechanism. In the same way that John Bonham or Dave Grohl or Mo Tucker are such powerfully steady drummers that the rest of the band is allowed to go completely off the rails without losing the plot, the unflappable consistency of Lou's sedated voice and barely varying chords (D and G, with a low D note ringing out for all eternity) are the foundational downbeat vibe that makes great heights of intensity possible for the other players. *That's* why David Bowie could belt out backing vocals at the top of his range behind "Satellite of Love" and not come off like an over-the-top embarrassment. Because Lou was grounding him in an immovable cool. That grounding may have been what made Bowie's entire bombastic career possible, the reason he (in the mid-sixties attempting a strange, whimsical folk-rock) didn't find success until he came under the influence of the Velvet Underground. Reed is so firmly rooted in realism—musical, lyrical, and personal—that his influence is a launching pad and landing strip for all types of cloud-chasing dreamers who otherwise might have drifted off into absurdity.

The song ends with a mighty crash. The crowd of drunk hipsters is worshipful. Lou Reed places his guitar on its stand and surveys the masses, not smiling but—we imagine— probably feeling *something*, right? We know he's supposed to be the detached observer. All day he's been taking photographs of the other bands, managing to seem apart even from this Lou-Reed-focused event, just documenting it without comment or real involvement. But can he remain emotionless at this moment, in front of a crowd of people who adore him, at the end of a day entirely dedicated to a celebration of his achievements by musicians whose lives he changed forever?

Suddenly he seems about to cry. He takes the microphone off the stand and speaks into it, slowly and emphatically, his weathered voice containing the barest emotional quiver: "I. Love. Punk Rock."

The audience somehow doubles its already frantic enthusiasm. Then Lou raises a fist in the air and says, "And I was the first one!"

He basks in the waves of love for a minute. Then he puts the mic back and leaves. The night is over.

* * *

I love punk rock, and I was the first one.

I found this line, the one thing Lou Reed had to say at his coronation as king of the hipsters, kind of surprising, kind of . . . off. Not what I would have expected.

First of all, I wouldn't have thought Lou Reed would have affirmed something as narrow as the genre label "punk rock." Being that the phrase didn't much exist until he'd already been in the rock 'n' roll game for at least ten years, being that "punk rock" was essentially a marketing term to describe mid-seventies bands influenced by him, many of whom he deeply disdained, it's a little weird to hear him claim it as his own like this. "The godfather of punk" is something a music writer would call him, not something he would call himself.

But more so, I think what was most jarring about it was that I'd never heard Lou Reed say anything so positive, so unambiguous. Every other time I've heard (or read) him speak, it's been in the form of insult, disavowal, grouchy retort, or noncommittal sidestep. That's his *whole thing*. He is, as Lester Bangs put it, "an emblem of absolute negativism."[1] All labels that the world offered up in reaction to him, he rejected or destabilized. Anything they expected of him, he refused to give them. He was against everything, even himself. From the beginning, he proclaimed it his mission: "I'm gonna try to nullify my life." His saying "no" to whatever they called him was an intentional act of self-destruction, and simultaneously an act of independence.

Which ultimately is why it's true that he was the first punk. If, when the word "punk" came to describe the whole New York scene he preceded and helped make iconic, he spurned the descriptor and scorned the genre as a collection of cheap imitators, even so, *all the more so* can it be used to refer to him. In its deepest sense, the word "punk" is a name for people who refuse all identities foisted on them by others. It is the identity that rejects all identity, the Blank Generation. A legion of Transformers, who are never finished changing, who regard easily digested labels, convenient stand-ins for their actual inconvenient selves, as a form of authoritarianism.

In the end, Reed found a way to define himself after all: the artist who called for the rejection of all definitions. The final word is that there is no final word.

And if you thought there was, fuck you.

---

[1] "The Greatest Album Ever Made," originally published in March 1976 issue of *Creem*, compiled in *Psychotic Reactions and Carburetor Dung*, ed. Greil Marcus.

Enormous Thanks

to God, my rock and my redeemer, I-will-be-what-I-will-be.

to April Artz, who told me 33⅓ had put out an open call for submissions and suggested I write one.

to Will Callison, who talked with me endlessly and delightfully about Lou Reed and issues of identity, and convinced me to go through with submitting.

to my editor Michelle Chen, who made this book much better than it would have been.

to Rosemarie Wagner, my foundation, my co-conspirator, my darling.

to my manager Simon Taffe, a damn good friend and the secret hero of my whole public life.

to my parents, who have made and continue to make my life not only possible, but beautiful.

to Kat Bawden, who first played me the Velvet Underground.

Also available in the series